Mack & Leeann's Guide to
SHORT-TERM
MISSIONS

J. Mack &
Leeann Stiles

InterVarsity Press
Downers Grove, Illinois

InterVarsity Press
P.O. Box 1400, Downers Grove, IL 60515
World Wide Web: www.ivpress.com
E-mail: mail@ivpress.com

InterVarsity Press® *is the book-publishing division of InterVarsity Christian Fellowship/USA*®*, a student movement active on campus at hundreds of universities, colleges and schools of nursing in the United States of America, and a member movement of the International Fellowship of Evangelical Students. For information about local and regional activities, write Public Relations Dept., InterVarsity Christian Fellowship/USA, 6400 Schroeder Rd., P.O. Box 7895, Madison, WI 53707-7895.*

All Scripture quotations, unless otherwise indicated, are taken from the Holy Bible, New International Version®. NIV®. *Copyright* ©*1973, 1978, 1984 by International Bible Society. Used by permission of Zondervan Publishing House. All rights reserved.*

Cover photograph: ©*Lila Nakazawa/Photonica*

ISBN 0-8308-2269-0

Printed in the United States of America ∞

Library of Congress Cataloging-in-Publication Data

Stiles, J. Mack, 1956-
   Mack & Leeann's guide to short-term missions / J. Mack & Leeann Stiles.
      p. cm.
   Includes bibliographical references.
   ISBN 0-8308-2269-0 (pbk.)
      1. Short-term missions. 2. Stiles, J. Mack, 1956- 3. Stiles, Leeann. I. Title: Mack and Leeann's guide to short-term missions. II. Stiles, Leeann. III. Title.

BV2061 .S695 2000
266—dc21
                                                                                    00-033513

20	19	18	17	16	15	14	13	12	11	10	9	8	7	6	5	4	3	2	1
16	15	14	13	12	11	10	09	08	07	06	05	04	03	02	01	00			

We'd like to dedicate this book to our parents:
Joe and Nancy Stiles
Ernie and Ann Northcutt
who have given us a love for the world

Contents

Acknowledgments

We're grateful for the hundreds of students and staff who risked their lives with us on global projects over the years. We would like to thank the InterVarsity missions team that faithfully served us: Scott Bessenecker, Rich Henderson, Paula Harris, Chuck Ellis, John Kyle, Mary Fisher, and Dan and Shelby Harrison. We are grateful for our first team of Overseas Training Camp (OTC) directors, especially Susie Veon and David and Marian Jones. The International Fellowship of Evangelical Students (IFES) has shown us kindness from Hong Kong to Dar es Salaam, especially Doug and Marilyn Stewart and Lindsay Brown. Thanks to all Student Training in Missions (STIM) trainers, but especially Linda Olson and Steve Eyre.

Thanks to the numerous Kenyan pastors who have served us over the years. We are especially thankful for Samuel Ngarachu. Thanks to Pete and Ruth Cowles and Lib Marsh at Africa Inland Mission (AIM) and AIM Air. Special thanks to our friends Philip and Mary Kishoyian. Thanks to Joshua Wathanga, David Kariuki, Calisto Odede, David Oginde, John Kanja and all the staff with Fellowship of Christian Unions (FOCUS-Kenya) who served our project in Kenya.

We wish to thank many unnamed faithful friends in the Middle East, especially I. and V.

In Guatemala we would like to thank Steve Beam of Missionary Ventures. Thanks to Arturo Miranda and the Centro Linguistico Maya in Antigua, the Church of God in Trapachito and Sumolito, Pablo Raymundo and Tomas Gusaro. Thanks to the staff of Students International, especially Hector Pinto, Jeff Sprecher, Sam Moore and Roderijo Aceituno. Thanks to Nebaj missionaries Kris Repp, Ronnie and Vickie Fielden, and Sharon Rosenwald. We are particularly grateful for Mike and Terri McComb, with New Life League. We are also thankful for John Carmichael, with Viajes Al Sur.

There have been many InterVarsity Christian Fellowship staff who have traveled with us over the years on short terms, but we especially want to thank David and Kris Lawrence, Julie Hall, Greg and Linda Jobe, Anita McGill, Jeannie Musick, Brian and Joanne Parks, David and Angie McNeill, and Tracy Price. Thanks also to Steve Hayner, Barney Ford, Bob Fryling and Roger Anderson for their help and support. Thanks to Shannon Rowe and Catherine Bunge who provided help with our children. We are grateful for First Alliance, Lexington, Kentucky, and supporters Ted and Judy Callahan. Also thanks for the support of our new Alliance church plant: Quest Community Church, Lexington, and our pastor and his wife, Pete and Jackie Hise. And, as always, special thanks to our faithful editor, Andy Le Peau.

We wish to acknowledge a special debt to InterVarsity's Student Training in Missions (STIM), which has proved to be a treasure for missions and the church as well as InterVarsity Christian Fellowship. Most of chapters seven to eleven rely on our experience in working with STIM principles.

Introduction

As a husband and wife team we have directed short-term missions for fourteen years. We think it is the greatest privilege of our lives. We have seen people transformed for the kingdom with fresh force and power—both those short termers we have taken and those nationals who have hosted us. We've been changed too. We're excited to present what we've learned in the school of hard missionary knocks in this book.

We have written a book from our experience. Because of that, a few disclaimers are necessary. Some may think our stories are broad-ranging global encounters. But we are aware of how limited our experience is. We are hoping to direct an Asian short term, but we use few stories from Asia. Though we have directed (and dearly love) domestic short terms, our stories focus more on foreign short terms. But we do feel the principles of this book are applicable to Asian, domestic and most any crosscultural situation. It may require some translating, but, hey, you're going on a short term so you might as well get started. Also we need to point out that there are many definitions of short terms. But when we talk about short terms, we are focusing more on trips measured in months and weeks, not years.

This is not a how-to book either. We're not focusing on visa applications or what shots to get. There are thousands of travel guides that cover those issues and usually the directors of short terms have specific guidelines for their programs too. We want to present a book that helps us understand foundational principles of short terms. That's the focus of the first six chapters of this book. Chapters seven through eleven look into developing critical crosscultural skills, and chapters twelve through eighteen deal with specific needs short termers have. We hope this is helpful; it comes from our heart.

One other note: this book is by both of us. We both led the groups of students on the various trips we took, so the ideas and experiences you find in these pages are from the two of us. We also shared in the actual writing of the book. Sometimes one of us would draft a chapter and the other would revise. Sometimes it was the other way around. But for ease of reading, we have chosen to have the book written in Mack's voice. He is the "I" you will read about in the following pages, unless otherwise indicated by context.

1

The Risky Adventure

I SAT ON A ROUGH WOODEN STOOL AT A RICKETY TABLE EATING UGALI and sukumawiki[1] somewhere between Mombasa and Nairobi with my Masai friend, Philip Kishoyian. We had stopped at the Kenyan trucker's restaurant of choice because it served Kishoyian's favorite: goat stew. Blue paint chips from the furniture mixed with the red clay on the ground. The cashier sat on a stool too, but he was surrounded by a mesh wire cage. His need for protection didn't dawn on me until after the meal. As we began to eat, a large Kenyan truck driver approached me from behind and greeted me gruffly in Swahili. Kishoyian's eyes grew large with fear as the cafeteria went quiet. But when I answered with a polite greeting in Swahili, two things happened: Kishoyian's eyes went from fear to shock, and the truck driver slapped me on the back. Miraculously, I had spoken the few Swahili phrases Kishoyian taught me as if I was a native speaker. As I finished off Kishoyian's delicious goat stew (he had lost his appetite), we were able to share with our new friend the love of God.

Ah, life is sweetest when one brushes death. (Leeann suggested that it was only teeth I was going to miss brushing.) At any rate my encounter still reminds me of Paul's words:

> We always carry around in our body the death of Jesus, so that the life of Jesus may also be revealed in our body. For we who are alive are always being given over to death for Jesus' sake, so that his life may be revealed in our mortal body. (2 Cor 4:10-11)

It was not the last time that I thought about that passage.

In the Middle East it seems that much of the view of America is shaped by Hollywood. Hatem, a Middle Eastern University student, told me in all seriousness that he thought most American men were like Rambo and most American women were like Madonna. (Do we export our best or what?) Furthermore, it was Hatem's view, until he befriended our group that summer, that most Americans would happily kill Arabs. I loved Hatem, and had no desire to do him in, but Hatem, a practical joker, had pulled stunts on some of our short termers that did produce a desire for friendly revenge.

Midway though our program Hatem introduced us to a beach where Muslim families could cavort without dealing with the decadence of European tourists.

"Come on, Hatem. Let's swim out to the sand bar," I said.

"No, I must take a cigarette. I will come as soon as I finish," he replied.

I leisurely swam toward the sand bar in the crystal-clear water while Hatem eased his nicotine fit. But in a few moments I spied Hatem swimming with broad strokes in the water underneath me. *He's trying to beat me to the sand bar,* I thought. *This is my chance!*

Before he broke the water's surface, I grabbed him from behind in a perfect chokehold. He sputtered and yelped, but I dunked him under. He thrashed about helplessly as I dunked him a second time. Laughing, I thrust him under a third time then spun him around by the shoulders.

Now it was my time to sputter—it wasn't Hatem! "Oh my," I stammered. "I'm so sorry. I thought you were someone else . . ."

He didn't speak English.

It didn't matter. My intentions and identity were clear enough: I was Rambo who came from America to his country to kill him personally. Coughing, he paddled backwards, never taking his eyes off me. I splashed after him continuing my moronic apologies "Dear me, you see . . . I'm so sorry," I repeated, but my attempts only seemed to cause more panic. Then I noticed his family gathering on the shore, thirty or forty strong.

Headlines passed before my eyes: "Arab Mob Kills American Terrorist!" But before I was *done in,* the real Hatem intervened. Slowly I realized that the family was not leering at me with bloodlust but laughing over our case of mistaken identity. Though the young man I dunked slipped off the premises never to be seen by me again, most of his family wanted to meet me. There are actual advantages to looking foolish rather than like Sylvester Stallone.

I can say, along with Paul:

If any one of you thinks he is wise by the standards of this age, he should become a "fool" so that he may become wise. For the wisdom of this world is foolishness in God's sight. (1 Cor 3:18-19)

*   *   *

The conditions of the rundown trailer park for migrant workers outside Tampa, Florida, seemed worse than the slums we visit in Guatemala. Our job was to go door to door distributing food and clothing, and telling people about the services of the Good Samaritan Mission. My ten-year-old son and I knocked on the dilapidated trailer door. I didn't notice the spray paint on the outside walls with the words "Latin Kings" until four muscular guys answered the door with scowls and suspicious looks, holding objects behind their backs. "Hola," I said, at precisely the same moment I realized this was the Latin King gang's headquarters. Tristan stood in front of me. My hands on his shoulders tensed; I wanted to pull him back and run. But Tristan, unaware, began telling them in Spanish why we were there. They brightened and smiled at the sound of his sweet natural Spanish (it was not the last time I felt thankful for Maxwell Elementary Spanish Immersion School). One gang member came outside with us. I had Tristan ask if he would like for us to read to him the gospel presentation we had brought with us. "Sí," he said, and he sat down in the dust. I speak little Spanish, but as I heard the gospel presented with a child's cadence to a Latin King gang member, apparently illiterate, I listened to a bigger thing going on: Tristan looked so small and impotent next to the large gang member; but "a little child shall lead them" was God's wisdom, not mine. When one of our group, Allen Bonnell, picked up this man that night and brought him to our church service, I was not surprised when he gave his life to Christ. Not surprised because I've found over time that when we risk—our pride, our time, our money, even our very lives—God works, no matter how childlike we look.

*   *   *

These experiences—from Africa to the inner city of America—help me say confidently today that short-term missions take us to places where risks for the gospel are rewarded with opportunities to build the kingdom—a world where those small risky steps of faith in God's hands become giant leaps of learning, growth and glory to God. After all, if God can use Tristan to bring a Latin King gang member to himself, he can use you and me.

I confess. We didn't start on short terms with such confidence. In fact, when Leeann and I agreed to direct an African short-term missions program years ago, it felt as if we risked everything for that trip: our careers, our lives and the safety of our new baby, Tristan. And the glare from this risk hid the joy and wonder God had in store for us.

The fact is we started ingloriously.

Leeann called me from the bathroom. (She was six months pregnant with Tristan and spent lots of time there.)

"Mack."

"Uh-huh," I responded from the just-awake-but-still-in-bed stage. I wasn't recovering from late nights of college ministry as quickly as I used to now that I was fifteen years older than the first-year students.

"I think the Lord really does want us to go."

"Really," I said. She didn't need to tell me what she was talking about. I knew.

"Yeah, I guess so," she said.

I leaned out of the bed to see her in the bathroom.

Tears dripped off her nose onto her opened Bible on the floor.

Events of the two previous weeks would prove to change our lives in undreamed of ways. We struggled during those weeks. We felt fear, forbidding and a bit of excitement. But our hearts knew. This was like the God we read about in Scripture. It was like him to "rudely" interrupt our plans and ideas about how we ran our lives. So without saying another word, I rolled over and punched the numbers on the phone.

"Good morning . . . Yes, John Kyle, please. Yes, I'll just wait."

John, the director of the Urbana Student Mission Convention, had happened to town and while there asked Leeann and me to pray about directing a short-term missions program in Kenya.

My first response was more a snort than a laugh. John couldn't be serious, and certainly there was no need to pray. Oh, I could quote Matthew 28:18 with the best of them, but to actually go . . . well, that was another thing. Not only were we going to have our first baby (didn't that disqualify us from taking radical steps for Jesus?), we didn't know a thing about Africa. How could I ask my pregnant wife to deliver our firstborn, then a few weeks later travel three thousand miles to a land neither of us had seen, to a people we did not know, who spoke a language we did not speak, to direct twenty students more frightened than we were?

But John was serious, and worse, the Holy Spirit seemed serious too. As unique as my objections felt, I knew we didn't have to travel far in the Scriptures to see we were on familiar territory with God.

The call from God to Abram was to "leave your country, your people and your father's household and go to the land I will show you" (Gen 12:1).

Abram left behind his native land, his culture and his family to go to a land they knew little about, a land of different values and culture and language. Yet Abram obeyed. In fact, his obedience is so simply stated that sometimes we skip over the costs, but they are just as real as ours when God calls us to go to other places today.

"Yes, hello John. It's Mack here. Well, I've got to admit that I'm surprised to be telling you that we would like to take you up on the offer to direct the short-term program to Kenya if the offer is still open . . . ."

Leeann's tears ran down her cheeks.

"Yes, the baby is due in January, and . . . uh-huh . . . ."

I paused to look up at Leeann.

"Yes, you told me before that our baby will do better in Africa than the students will . . . uh-huh."

I didn't mention to him that worrying about our students hadn't even started. I was unashamedly worried about us.

"Yes, God is faithful . . . Okay, John, thanks."

When I hung up the phone, Leeann said, "Well, we're in."

Boy, were we in. Of course, what we thought we were into and what we actually were into turned out to be very, very different. We thought that we had signed up to do missions work for God in Africa. And that was true, but God had some very different ideas about what that meant. That's the story of the following chapter.

2

The First Journey
From Head to Heart

DURING THIS YEAR THOUSANDS WILL VENTURE ON A SHORT TERM somewhere in the world. Short-term mission participants range from cooks and mechanics to doctors and lawyers, from high school youth groups to retired people, from students to stay-at-home moms.

Today there is scarcely a missions agency, church or parachurch organization that does not send short-term missionaries downtown or around the globe—and for a growing number of parachurch organizations the only work they do is short terms. Few predicted this movement even twenty years ago. What is going on?

Part of the reason for the growth of short terms is simply because we can. Airplanes whisk us away for visits that would have been impossible for missions years ago. Our short-term programs happen in the same amount of time it took to *travel* to those destinations in the early 1900s. Many dub air travel the modern equivalent of the Roman roads, noting the parallels of our ease of travel to the ease of travel Paul had on trade routes in his day.

Another reason exists for the growth of short-term missions. In the 1970s and 1980s a top-selling Christian book was *Knowing God*. In the 1990s a top-selling Christian book was *Experiencing God*. Though the shift in titles may seem subtle—displacing one similar verb for another—it speaks to a profound cultural shift. We desire our relationship with God to go beyond an academic faith; we want to have more than head knowledge in our walk with God; we want to experience God.

Kristi wrote in her journal after our short term in the Middle East, "I discovered God didn't take a flight on my 747 to get here. He's been working here long before I came. . . . I experienced a bigger God than I ever knew existed."

We live in a culture that reminds us daily that if you want something done, you'd better do it yourself—trust your own plan. And so gradually, imperceptibly, Christians absorb this cultural sea in which we swim, but we can never experience God on our own terms. On a short term we put our faith on the line. The cultural props that go with a life under control are stripped from us. And it's there that we experience God most clearly. To experience God we must give up the control we crave.

The place God wants us to start in missions work is not to get a passport, buy a plane ticket or develop vacation Bible school curriculum. The place to start is by recognizing that you must trust God's plan and not your own. The short-term missions trip is an instrument God uses to help Christians learn to trust him in deeper and profound ways.

We ran our first program in Kenya cookbook style—relying on the notes from those who had directed the program before us. Each morning of our first week, we poured over the teaching for that day while experiencing an awaking Africa: mules braying, cocks crowing and the smell of burning garbage.

During that time we taught a session on the Great Commission. It was a bright African morning, and I was preparing my talk. But the crushing responsibilities, the shock of a new culture and my own sense of unworthiness made me feel as if I had descended into the heart of darkness. I wasn't sure I could do the teaching. I wasn't sure I could do this project, period! I sat paralyzed with an open Bible before me.

This is the passage I stared at that Kenyan morning:

All authority in heaven and on earth has been given to me. Therefore go and make disciples of all nations, baptizing them in the name of the Father and of the Son and of the Holy Spirit, and teaching them to obey everything I have commanded you. And surely I am with you always, to the very end of the age. (Mt 28:18-20)

Up to then I thought of these verses as the missionary-pitch passage, something people used to motivate people for missions. The missionary motivators read this passage with an emphasis on the middle text, while the first and last parts of this text are read as afterthoughts. Like this:

All authority in heaven and on earth has been given to me. There-fore go and make disciples of all nations, baptizing them in the name of the Father and of the Son and of the Holy Spirit, and teaching them to obey everything I have commanded you. And surely I am with you always, to the very end of the age.

Yet there I was in "all nations." It was there that I found myself reading these Scriptures for the first time like this:

All authority in heaven and on earth has been given to me. Therefore go and make disciples of all nations, baptizing them in the name of the Father and of the Son and of the Holy Spirit, and teaching them to obey everything I have commanded you. And surely I am with you always, to the very end of the age.

It was as if Jesus had sprung from the pages of the Bible, grabbed me by the lapels and spoke forcefully in my face: "I love you. I'm in charge. You're in the middle of the Great Commission, now believe the two ends of this passage. I have all authority and I'm going with you—forever!"

This may not seem a great revelation. There are few who could not parrot this bit of theology. Imagine the yawns if we came back from Africa and reported, "We did a lot of exciting things, but the best part of our trip was learning God was faithful." But to have experienced it, deeply, profoundly, when it felt as if our life was on the line was worth the price of the trip. We discovered the eighteen-inch journey from head to heart was even longer than the journey from home to the heart of Africa.

That summer we began to experience God as bigger than the challenges of foreign logistics, bigger than the frustrations of cultural differences and, yes, bigger than the fears we had of taking a new baby to a new place. God is in charge. He is faithful to his word. He goes with us.

Our responsibilities didn't decrease that summer, but we sensed God's presence, and we trusted Jesus to do what he said he would do. He called us, after all—it was his problem. We started living the Great Commission.

The day came to return home from our first short term. This

was the day we dreamed about even before we left. And, gloriously, we would return with as many participants as we took— the low bar of success on a missions trip. Yet when we stepped off the plane in drab JFK Airport, we felt overwhelmed with sadness. As we watched the short termers make their way through the terminal for their flights home, we realized that despite our inexperience, God worked wonders in their hearts, we made a difference in some Kenyan lives, and we experienced the faithfulness of Jesus. We wanted to go back; we wanted to do it again.

One of the first phone calls was to John Kyle.

"John? Mack and Leeann here . . . Yes, we had a wonderful time . . . Yes, he *is* faithful, isn't he? . . . Right, well, we were actually wondering if we might sign up for next year."

3

Abraham's Math Lesson
A Missions Mindset

"The Scripture foresaw that God would justify the Gentiles by faith,
and announced the gospel in advance to Abraham:
'All nations will be blessed through you.' "

GALATIANS 3:8

GOD PULLED ABRAM OUT OF HIS TENT DURING THE MIDDLE OF THE night somewhere in the rocky hill country near Hebron for a math lesson.

"Abram, count the stars."

Astronomers tell us that on a clear night you can see thousands of stars, and most nights in the desert are startlingly clear. I wonder, how long did God let Abram count? How many hours did Abram sit on a warm rock in the cool desert night and try and calculate the number of tiny, shimmering lights above him?

We know Abram (later to be renamed *Abraham*) obediently left everything—home lands, family, religion—at the command of the Lord, so it's easy to picture him fulfilling this simple request with unhesitating devotion:

"One, two, three, four, five, six . . ."

Abram counting stars crafts an image the world has never forgotten. Not bad for just one night of lost sleep. Besides, the questions crowding Abram's mind didn't allow for restful sleep:

When will I have a child?

How will God fulfill his promise to me?

My wife is old—maybe I should get a younger woman?

God knew counting can be therapeutic for sleepless nights. But plans to soothe Abram's worries seem small compared to God's plan to use Abram to change the world.

"Two thousand and seventy-seven, two thousand and seventy-eight, two thousand and seventy . . ."

When the sun's rise made it no longer possible for Abram to count stars, God gave Abram the point: "So shall your offspring be" (Gen 15:5).

God is reemphasizing what he had previously told Abram, "*All peoples on earth* will be blessed through you" (Gen 12:3, my emphasis).

Abram's sleepless night turned out to be more than a math lesson, it was even more than the reassurance of a child, it was a picture of God's heart. Through *Abraham* God reveals his plan for the world. God wanted Abraham to have a missions mindset. He wants us to have one too.

Long before Jesus uttered the Great Commission to his disciples, God displayed his missionary heart. If the place to start in short-term missions is to trust God's plan, as we said in the last chapter, then the first thing to understand about missions is that it's a part of God's character—God has a missions mindset.

In fact, from the first pages of the Bible to the very last, we see God consistently state his concern for the world. God gave provisions for outsiders in the law of Moses; kings were rebuked for the mistreatment of aliens; prophets were sent to foreign countries; foreigners were even included in the family tree of Jesus. Though the *ways* of other cultures—especially religions that included child sacrifice and religious orgies—were soundly condemned (but seldom heeded), the love for those who would embrace the Lord are just as plainly stated. Over and again God declares his concern and compassion for the nations with a love that will culminate on a day pictured for us in the last book of the Bible, when there will be "a great multitude that no one could count, *from every nation, tribe, people and language*" (Rev 7:9, my emphasis) before the throne of God.

The sad thing is how quickly and easily the Israelites missed the point God made to Abraham and the prophets. They *never* practiced God's missionary heart—just the opposite—they twisted the doctrine of election into a racist system that excluded the nations.

Is it any wonder then that when Jesus, the King of kings and the Lord of all nations, arrived triumphantly on Palm Sunday for what should have been his coronation in the city of Jerusalem, and marched up the steps of the temple, the rulers refused to crown him king? They didn't even see him as a good man.

Jesus' first act was not to kneel to be crowned at the temple, but to fall on the moneygrubbers who profited from swindling aliens and foreigners—the irony completely missed by those in charge. His rage came not only from the injustice and idolatry that comes from mixing greed and religion, but from the theft of God's intent for his house.

After Jesus chased the hucksters away he quoted the forgotten verse: " 'My house will be called a house of prayer *for all nations.'* But you have made it 'a den of robbers' " (Mk 11:17, my emphasis).

By missing God's heart for the nations they missed the blessing—they missed Jesus.

It's not enough to point our fingers at the children of Israel. I find uncomfortable parallels in the modern church and its understanding of missions. We need a missions mindset too. To exclude missions excludes us from God's heart: a heart for the nations. Without a missionary mindset we too give in to the mix of greed and religion. Without a missionary mindset the church can easily fall into a racist understanding of the world. Without a missionary mindset we miss Jesus.

So what is the missionary mindset? A missionary mindset understands God's love for all people of every ethnicity and culture. A missionary mindset is a rock-solid belief that Jesus is Savior, Lord and Hope of the world. Furthermore, the missionary mindset understands that to live out God's heart, every Christian must move across barriers and differences to extend his message of love and salvation to all people, despite the odds or cost. All Christians should have a missionary mindset, even if all Christians won't be missionaries.

We want to suggest four things that frame a missionary mindset; four things to start your short term and stay with you for the rest of your life.

A Missions Mindset Knows That Jesus Is Lord

Jesus said, "I am the way and the truth and the life. No one comes to the Father except through me" (Jn 14:6).

In a pluralistic age, to make an exclusive claim (or even to believe in an exclusive claim) is seen as ignorant at best and dangerous at worst. This is an age of tolerance. But not only do we make an exclusive claim about Jesus, we act it out by moving to other lands proclaiming our convictions that Jesus is the Lord of the universe. Though we respect other faiths and acknowledge that there is some truth in all religion, we present Jesus as the only way. We ask people to turn in faith to Jesus. We say this knowing full well how out of sorts it is with the world around us. Left to ourselves we wouldn't say it at all, but we follow Jesus as Lord, and he claimed this truth about himself, and he asks us to proclaim his truth today. That's the point. It's not that we love to tell others that their faith won't get them to God, it's that Jesus said he knows the way, the only way. Jesus is not sanctimonious or narrow; he is the way of God's mercy and love. Unless we are sure of this conviction, our faith will be weak in the face of opposition, conflict and cost, and our missions will be bankrupt.

This is not only a missions concern, of course. Ultimately there is no reason to take a stand for Christ anywhere if you believe Jesus is a good option among many, be it an angry Marxist in Central America, a clever professor in the classroom or the raised eyebrows of coworkers. But believing Jesus is the way, the truth and the life is why we take a stand for him in the midst of a pluralistic culture.

A Missions Mindset Understands That Missions Is the Responsibility of Every Christian

Paul says, "Everyone who calls on the name of the Lord will be saved" (Rom 10:13). Then he begins a series of rhetorical questions designed for us to see our role.

First: *"How, then, can they call on the one they have not believed in?"* (Rom 10:14).

(They can't.)

Next: *"And how can they believe in the one of whom they have not heard?"* (Rom 10:14).

(They can't.)

Finally, *"And how can they hear without someone preaching to them?"* (Rom 10:14).

(They won't.)

Could Paul have had in mind the missionary question that confronted Isaiah when the Old Testament prophet stood before the throne of God and heard, "Whom shall I send? And who will go for us?" (Is 6:8)?

A call from God's heart is issued, and we have the opportunity to take part. Paul gives that call to us as believers to become a missionary people. His question floats in the air for us, "How will they hear?"

Our answer? "Here am I; send me" (Is 6:8). "I want to be a part of what you are doing. I want to be a part of your plan. I don't want to miss Jesus."

We take part in missions because God is a missionary God, and he calls his people to be missionary people. Just as God's concern is for the whole world, so should we have a concern for the whole world.

A Missions Mindset Calls People to Move Out

Wonderful things happen on short terms, but they don't happen if people don't go. After God told Abraham to leave his country and people and go to another land, God also told him, "I will bless you" (Gen 12:2). But too many want the blessing without leaving.

In the New Testament Paul makes it clear that we are now the spiritual heirs of Abraham and have inherited the missionary promises to Abraham (Gal 3:1-18)—including the blessing.

The blessings from missions defy listing. I mentioned in the last chapter how Leeann and I discovered God's faithfulness in our lives. We are stretched; we grow, we see new things on a short-term missions trip. We discover the breadth of God's love and the depth of our need. We get a fresh view of our own situation and culture that we wouldn't have if we didn't leave it. We're allowed to do ministry. We come home with an understanding of people different from ourselves, even if they live next door.

It's apparent to many ministers and youth workers that they can do in a few short weeks on a missions trip what it often takes years to do back home in the comfort zone of church.

Brian Sanders spoke to me after directing his first Urban Project, in Tampa, Florida.

"Mack," he said, "I can't believe how much happened in the lives of the people who were there. I think I saw four years of ministry happen on our four-week program."

Time and again we see truth in the cliché that "we get more than we give." People who attend a program with the intention to give find that they receive more back.

Be warned: there is a danger here. The spiritual blessings of short terms may be habit-forming. But they do not come if you do not go.

A Missions Mindset Knows God Uses All People to Change the World—Even You

Just as when Abraham sat on a rock and fretted while God desired to use him to change the world, we too can let our concerns blind us from seeing God's bigger plans working though us. Sometimes it's hard to believe we can be a part of Abraham's blessing for the whole world. But God will do the work if we take the steps, because we have inherited that part of the promise to Abraham too. Paul says, "He redeemed us in order that the blessing given to Abraham might come to the Gentiles through Christ Jesus" (Gal 3:14). We are now the spiritual heirs of Abraham. We are the result of the promise; we can be a part of seeing his promise happen in other people's lives.

So we invite the world to wonder and marvel with us about God. John Piper says, "Missions exists because [there are places where] worship doesn't."[1]

We also extend his message of liberating love. Most of the world thinks that somehow they must earn the right to be children of God, and we have the privilege to tell them that simple faith in Christ allows access to God! One does not have to be born to the right parents, gifted with a high IQ or clothed in the right skin to get to God. It's simple faith in Jesus.

I sat with Mike high in the Guatemalan mountains on a bluff. Mike shook his head for the third time. "No, Mack . . . I just don't think I have anything to share. What can I say to these people?"

On our left, built into the mountainside, lay a Mayan earthen shrine to the local mountain deity. On our right ran a trench that had housed a machine-gun nest a few short years before. The town behind us was a poor village called Trapachito. Mike picked a blade of grass and studied it.

"Mike, I won't make you share, but remember you can read, and these people can't. You offer so much, even if it's just to read a passage of Scripture . . . Mike, God will use you."

I felt for Mike. He was a young Christian and like most was stunned by the poverty. Mike took a breath. "Well, okay. But it'll be short."

"That's fine with me," I said.

That night we gathered in a small church building built lovingly from rough pine planks. Six or seven locals were there— almost all the Christians in that village. As they gathered, they seemed weary and dispirited. We later discovered that people in their village were threatening to run them out of town for their faith.

I stood, bumping my head against the bottom of a kerosene candle that burned over the pulpit. The shadows in the room swayed back and forth. As I steadied the bottle, I said, "Brother

Mike has a word for us tonight."

Mike stood, a bit too quickly, and made his way to the pulpit. He held his small Bible close in the dark and nervously read this passage of Scripture from Matthew:

> The kingdom of heaven is like a mustard seed, which a man took and planted in his field. Though it is the smallest of all your seeds, yet when it grows, it is the largest of garden plants and becomes a tree, so that the birds of the air come and perch in its branches. (Mt 13:31-32)

Mike waited for the translation. Then he gave a sermon, repeated here in its entirety.

"You guys and I have something in common," he said. "We're new to faith. But Jesus said that he can take even a small amount of faith and make big things happen. I know that's true in my life. He takes our faith, just like a small seed, and makes it grow. I think that's going to happen with this church. You may feel as small as a seed right now, but remember God is going to make big things happen here—big things for his kingdom."

Mike never took his eyes off the ground during his sermon, but at the end he looked around the room and said, "Thanks." And shuffled back to his seat.

Because the sermon was so short, I felt compelled to add some more teaching, but I needn't have bothered. Mike's words struck straight and true. It was a word from God for those people. Later that night Pablo preached (we had lots of sermons that night), and a man gave his life to Jesus.

When we visited that church four years later, it was in the same building, but the building was now too small to hold the vibrant fellowship of twenty families—close to half of the village—and growing. Mike's words proved prophetic.

Every time I visit the church in Trapachito, they ask about "that preacher, Miguel. You know," they say, "the one who brought us a word from the Lord."

Mike made a difference—not based on his biblical studies or his preaching skills, but because he has a great God who uses people like him and Abraham and you. The story of missions is a story about people making a difference because they had faith the size of a mustard seed that God grew into a big work. Remember Mike's words: "You may feel as small as a seed right now, but remember God is going to make big things happen here—big things for his kingdom."

When we develop a missions mindset, big things happen—be it on a short term or at home. That's because God made Abraham a promise that Abraham's sons and daughters inherited—you and I. When we move out and proclaim Jesus as Lord in whatever place he has called us to be, God, in his economy, can use us even in our weakness to change the world.

4

Models for Modern Short Terms

WE HAVE A GUY LIKE HERB ON EVERY SHORT TERM: A LINEAR THINKER in a nonlinear missions world. Herb complained for two days about how poorly we were digging the muck out of a fish-farm pond. (An orphanage sold the fish and used the proceeds for funding, but that's another story.) Finally, partly out of concern for Herb and partly because I couldn't take the complaining anymore, I sat Herb down.

"Mack, I know something about digging. I worked all summer on a ditch-digging crew," he said.

"Look, Herb," I said, ignoring his expertise, "this is not about efficiency or even digging up a pond. It's about other things. Like demonstrating servanthood—the Guatemalans can tell we're not doing it because we're *good* at it. If we wanted to be efficient, we would have taken the money you raised, left you behind and hired some Guatemalan workers to do in two hours what it's taken our whole group to do in two days. Herb, we're not here for efficiency, or anything else you can readily measure, we're here to demonstrate the love of Jesus."

Short-term missions advocates cite recent studies that show that when short-term people return, they support missions at almost double the level they did before and pray more specifically for those they visited.[1]

Short-term advocates tout other benefits, saying short terms have done much for helping raise missions consciousness too. A missionary friend says that after years of questions, she now supports short-term programs because of their impact in galvanizing missions awareness in the church. It's true; we see people's eyes opened to the global call of Christ around the world with every short term we direct.

Yet if it were a simple matter of efficiency, God would never use inefficient people to perform his plan, and we all know how costly that plan has been for him.

Frankly, most arguments I hear, both pro and con, about short terms are frustratingly limited. Sometimes we worry that these arguments come from insecurity, from a sense that short terms are second best. But our experience is that we don't have to justify short terms due to the good they do for long-term missions. They are good in and of themselves. They do powerful things for the kingdom—different from long terms—but equally viable.

That is not to say that there are not legitimate concerns about short terms. There are. We see short terms that make us cringe. Well, okay, we've made mistakes on our own short terms that make us cringe. The point being that for all the good arguments against short terms, they should not be seen as a call for the end of short-term missions (or the end of support for short terms), rather as a corrective and stimulus for thoughtful and well-prepared short-term programs. So where do we look for models?

There are striking parallels in both the Old and New Testaments with modern short terms. Jonah, who has been included in many a missionary talk, was a short termer. His easily translated message of eight words happened over the course of three days (plus a debriefing of thirty-seven days). The first missionary work in the early church, Peter's visit to the Gentiles at the house of Cornelius (Acts 10), lasted no longer than a week and certainly constitutes a short term. (We will study Peter's short term as a model in future chapters.)

Another model of short terms comes from the missionary work of Paul. What most marks my mind about Paul's travels are the powerful miracles, the growth of the church and the bravery of those proclaiming Christ. But look carefully at the less flashy but quite revealing time frame of Paul's journeys. F. F. Bruce notes that the church in Antioch commissioned Paul and Barnabas for missionary work in the spring of A.D. 48. Paul and Barnabas first visited Barnabas's home country of Cyprus, where they stayed for eight weeks. From there they journeyed by sea to Pamphylia for two weeks. Then, after traveling by land, they wintered in Iconium for four or five months.

In the spring of 49 they moved to Lystra and Derbe, where they stayed for fourteen weeks. In Derbe they probably celebrated the one-year anniversary of their departure from the home church in Antioch. From Derbe, Paul and Barnabas spent their summer retracing steps to encourage the new Christians and returned to Antioch, rejoicing, in the late summer of 49.[2]

In Paul's second missionary journey the travel itinerary reads much the same as the first. Travel stays to cities averaged three months. Churches (in Philippi and Thessalonica) were established in a matter of weeks.

Paul rarely stayed in a city longer than five months. A long stay for him was a year and a half[3] in the city of Corinth. Even then Paul would have left Corinth sooner had he not received a vision assuring him that the Lord has "many people in this city" (Acts 18:10).

Here's what is striking: except when imprisoned, Paul *only* did short-term missions. Paul practiced and directed short-term projects. That's a powerful biblical model for short-term missions.[4]

Paul not only models short terms simply by showing us that short terms can start something big, he demonstrates three important principles that should be included in every short term.

Short Termers Need a Larger Biblical Picture of Missions

Paul understood the bigger biblical picture. However, many short termers remain clueless about the larger biblical picture of missions.

Even non-Christians see the benefit of traveling to unique and unusual places to help the disadvantaged, while expanding their world. This mindset, though, is the very reason a biblical understanding of missions is blurred. Today it is easy to go on a missions program without knowing why you are there, much less having a firm biblical understanding of why we go. One of the biggest problems facing the church about short-term missions is a foundational problem: many people involved in missions are missing God's heart for the world.

"Angie, tell me, why did you come here?" I asked during the break at language school.

Angie immediately launched into a discussion about how she

had been interested in Central America since she had taken some Spanish classes and how her youth worker had recommended our program and that it fit well with her summer schedule. She then topped off her response with a brief cost analysis of comparative programs. I felt as if Angie had picked up the latest copy of *Consumer Missions Quarterly* and picked a best buy.

"But Angie," I said. "Why come on a short term at all?"

She replied, "I think that God wants me to find his will for my life here."

"Okay, Angie, so the point of the trip is for you to come to Guatemala and find out God's will for your life?"

"Yeah," said Angie sensing a trap. "I guess so."

"But, is that the point of missions?" I asked.

"It is for me," she said with a smile.

I'm not saying that Angie won't discover God's will for her life in missions on short terms. In fact, if a person is considering becoming a missionary, it makes sense to try out missions before going long term, but to do that without hearing a biblical perspective of God's heart for the world is a disservice to the nations and destructive to missions.

While we have presented the biblical foundations for short-term missions in chapter three and in this chapter, there is a list of biblical references in the "Short Terms A—Z" section at the end of this book (under *biblical basis of missions*) for more in-depth study. It is important to have this foundation for short-term missions.

Short Termers Need to Understand Cultural Sensitivity

Paul understood the need for cultural sensitivity. Paul said, "I have become all things to all men so that by all possible means I might save some" (1 Cor 9:22). Paul's break from Jewish tradition was a radical model of understanding the need for cultural sensitivity.

Though most all Western short termers mean well, our notions tend to color our world too brightly for us to distinguish subtle cultural innuendoes—or even not-so-subtle innuendoes. We need to understand the difference between biblical truth and cultural understandings. Consider this story:

Kim, fresh out of Guatemalan customs at the airport and uncomfortably packed on the brightly colored bus bound for our training site, asked, "Mack, where are the guys that put the luggage on top of the bus?"

"They're up on top too," I said.

"Isn't that dangerous?" she asked

"It's incredibly dangerous," I answered.

"Tell them to get down," she directed.

"Kim, we can't get off the plane and start telling people what to do. This isn't our culture. That's how they do things here."

Good-hearted desires to immediately put things right are exactly the wrong way to develop cultural sensitivity. (Of course, a couple of students wanted to ride on top with the guys, which is a different problem.)

This is so important that chapters seven through eleven of this book are devoted to cultural sensitivity.

Short Termers Need to Form a Long-Term View

One missionary friend of mine complained, "Mack, if you're called to be a brain surgeon, you don't do it on a short-term basis; you devote your life to it. If you are unwilling to devote your life to missions, you won't do that very well either." Yet Paul came home to go to other places. In today's world we need a long-term view of missions—even short terms.

Understanding that short terms have strong biblical foundations, combined with an understanding of God's heart for the world, a desire to be culturally sensitive and a long-term view go a long way to make sure short terms are effective and biblical missionary work. Our next chapter deals with some ways to develop a long-term view of short-term misssions. Paul didn't return to Antioch thinking he had done his missionary deal. He actively looked for openings to return and take others with him. He maintained contact with the churches he planted for the remainder of his life. He had a long-term view. We need one too.

5

Short Terms with a Long-Term View

"HI LEEANN, THIS IS STEPHANIE, FROM KENYA LAST YEAR?"

Almost every year we get a phone call similar to this one from Stephanie. A student from the University of Arizona, Stephanie went on the previous year's summer trip to Kenya. She stayed with a young Kenyan pastor in the desperately poor area of West Pokot. He and his wife had no running water and no electricity, but he pastored three vibrant and growing churches. Stephanie's short term transformed her.

"I think that last summer was the hardest, most wonderful thing I've ever done in my life, so wonderful, in fact, I was wondering if you let people go again with you on your short term?" she asked.

"*Let* people?" Leeann responded, "We love it!"

It didn't start that way. At first Leeann and I discouraged people from returning on our program. After all, once you've been on a short term, you've done your part. Besides, why would you want to do basically the same thing again next year when you could see the world on different short terms? But the questions for return trips kept coming with such regularity that we began to wonder, "Why don't we let people go again?"

We see now that our thinking reflected a general conception of short terms as a one-time deal: you go, you come home, and you've done your part for missions. We had a short-term mindset about short terms. But as we returned year after year to the same place, we began to notice that our experiences were vastly different from year to year even though we were in the same place. We made deeper friendships with people, and their impact on us was greater too. And we noticed our time in Kenya seemed less distant when we returned home. Why couldn't the same thing happen for those who wanted to return? Our decision to return to Kenya for many summers helped us understand that we needed a long-term view of short-term missions.

Willow Creek Community Church has developed a helpful model of evangelism for busy people in modern life. It's the simple principle of returning to the same place or person for the repetitive things you do. So you get in the same bank line for the same teller, or you get to know the same cashier at the grocery store. Through short encounters over time, you look for opportunities for personal connection, invitations and even openings to share the gospel. You trust that you are sowing seeds that you may or may not see come to fruition but that God will use. This is a long-term view in a fast-food world. We need the same mindset in short-term missions. We need long-term views of short-term missions.

If you are a participant in a short term, you also should consider going more than once to the same place. If you direct a program or sponsor one in your church, find a place to which you can return again and again rather than world-hopping.

The best thing about fostering short-term missions with a long-term view is to see God work over time.

It was the morning after our church service for the village of Trapachito where Mike preached his brief mustard seed sermon. A father approached me. His thirteen-year-old daughter, Maria, had been in the fields with him planting corn when a paralysis took away the movement from half her face.

"Please pray for her healing," he requested.

Her mouth had the look mine does when I've had a hefty shot of novocaine from the dentist. Her face was stained with tears.

We gathered the church in the shed for prayer. Pine needles still lay scattered on the dirt floor as an aromatic carpet and reminded us of the service we celebrated the night before. We laid hands on Maria and prayed. Nothing happened, except Maria reported that she heard a ringing in her ears. That seemed worse to me, but it was time to leave.

During that year I would pray for Maria and her father, his anguished face etched into my memory.

The following year we returned. We heard reports about the gospel moving in that small village. The church had doubled in a year, and the believers were encouraged. After hiking to town and greeting the people we had met the previous year, I asked, "How is Maria, the young girl who had a problem with her face?"

"Oh," they looked up as if trying to remember something, then said, "Maria's fine, of course—remember you prayed that she would be healed." They certainly had more faith in my prayers than I.

Within minutes they produced Maria. She stood before me with a broad, shy smile.

And my faith was increased. I praised God for his goodness—something I would have missed if I had not returned.

Paul wanted to go back too. His first missionary journey is recorded in Acts 13; his second missionary journey starts in Acts 15. But Paul's second missionary journey might be best thought of as a continuation of the first. His second trip probably happened a year or two after the first. Here's how it happened:

> Some time later Paul said to Barnabas, "Let us go back and visit the brothers in all the towns where we preached the word of the Lord and see how they are doing." (Acts 15:36)

That's it: "Let us go back and visit." Paul simply longed to see how the new Christians were doing. And so the second missions trip was born. Paul's repeat trip was follow-up work: a follow-up to his first short term. The concerns on his heart included a specific teaching from the Jerusalem church[1] and to make sure that they remained strong in the faith.

Paul's revisit sprang from his concern for the people he met on his short term and his love for Christ. As he said to the Corinthians, "For Christ's love compels us, because we are convinced that one died for all, and therefore all died" (2 Cor 5:14).

Paul knew that a one-time sensational swing through town, ending with a marvelous debriefing talk to the Jerusalem church, however successful, was not enough. The apostle's desire to revisit should mark our short-term mission trips today. As one missionary friend of mine commented, "For me the distinction between good and bad short terms is not how much 'wow' there is on the trip—it's just too easy to get caught up in the sensational—but how much love is grown in relationships."

Some churches and fellowships make decade-long commitments to a site that allows for two wonderful things to happen: relationships with nationals and greater cultural understanding. And over time the benefits will multiply. Here are nine ways we see how a long-term view helped our programs:

1. We offered better training for issues of cultural sensitivity. Because we had friendships with nationals, we were able to recruit nationals to tell us about their country during our orientation. As a result, we learned important instructions—such as how to catch a Matatu bus in Kenya, what to wear on a Muslim beach, or what sermons had impact for the Ixil people.

2. We made better choices of who would best fit on our programs. Our program in Kenya required a willingness to live ruggedly. In the Middle East our accommodations were comfortable, but we required a higher spiritual maturity. Our hikes in the Guatemalan mountains required physical stamina. These are things we found out by going back over time, and we were better able to determine who should go.

3. We focused on people, not place. The Lord says taste and see that the Lord is good (Ps 34:8), not taste the good world to see the Lord. A long-term mindset encourages ongoing personal relationships rather than wanderlust. It puts task secondary to relationships. When you are in one place for a long time, the lure of the exotic wears off. We gently but firmly resist short-term missions that are cleverly disguised vacations. Take a vacation if you wish, but to mix vacationing with missions sends a mixed message to the people to whom you go. Drink in the sights when they happen, do not seek them out. This is a constant struggle in a place like Kenya, where game parks are all most Americans know. When we returned from Kenya, we were asked if we saw many animals. "Oh, yes," we would answer, "lots of cows, goats, sheep and dogs."

4. We fostered better evangelism. Short terms with a long-term view are much more sensitive to the specific issues facing evangelism for certain cultures. We'll devote chapter thirteen to this, but it's enough to say here that evangelism in another culture is much more complex than passing out tracts. And people feel freer to work on relationships knowing that they are part of an ongoing outreach.

5. We made long-term connections and friendships. The relationships we form on a short term can last a lifetime—just like Paul. When I walk down the streets of Antigua, Guatemala, where we do our training, I see people I know. People will stick their heads out of passing cars and say "Hola, Señor Mack!"

We have spent four summers there, and I keep going back to the same people, the same bus driver who takes our group to Nebaj, the same language school where we get all our students to take a stab at language learning. I see people I know who heard me give a talk in their church. Certainly not with the depth of a long-term missionary who lives there, but with a far greater ability than if I had only been once.

6. We enjoyed our building projects more because we got to see results. Over the years we've seen the Christian school in Nebaj grow. We helped pour the concrete wall one year, put in the latrine field the next, puttied in the glass windows and built the basketball court (my all-time favorite work project accomplishment). We've seen the school grow. The first year it was a shell; when we work there now, we have to work around all the kids who are in school. And we've built more than basketball courts; we've built relationships, because people saw our group year after year and appreciated that we had come back.

7. We saw bonding between short-term alumni. There is a bonding ability on short terms that I find in few other places in ministry. Even when participants don't go the same year, they find special connections with those who have gone another time. And they are able to keep in touch better by asking for news of families or people they met.

8. People learn skills on short terms that last a lifetime. One of the things we are most pleased to see back home is a greater awareness and concern for people who are different. Racist attitudes that were once seen as normal are challenged. People who might have been seen as frightening are seen as potential friends.

9. We have seen more people return for long term missions because of a long-term mindset. One of the best things for some about a long-term mindset is that it encourages and considers long-term missions.

After Michelle Woodberry joined us for her third trip to Kenya, there was something I needed to say: "Michelle, you're so good at this, I think you need to think about going long term."

"You know, I was thinking the exact same thing," she said with a smile.

Not long after that, she left her job to pursue a degree in missions, with plans to go overseas full-time.

A long-term view of short-term missions is a mindset that loves the people you've met and desires along with Paul to "*go back and visit.*"

6

Extra!
Would-Be Missionary Becomes Headhunter!

ONE YEAR A YOUNG FATHER AND HUSBAND, MICHAEL, JOINED OUR trip to Guatemala. He felt God's call on his life to the missions field at the Urbana Student Mission Convention and returned home from there with goals for missionary service.

Michael worked hard to get his pilot's license, hoping to become a support missionary in aviation. He enrolled in a Bible college, where he became president of the missionary society. He helped support his family, even taking on a paper route to make ends meet. But Michael felt he needed actual missions experience, so he joined our short-term program to Guatemala. It was a sacrificial act. Not only would Michael lose wages during the summer, but he would be away from his children and wife, Sue, who was pregnant with their third child. A generous family in their church provided Michael's support. The church commissioned him to go.

But despite the commissioning, five days into the short term Michael received an e-mail from a church leader summoning him home. Michael's wife, it seemed, had complications with her pregnancy.

He wrote:

> Michael, I am confident that you will not look back on your decision to return with any regrets. But you will have regrets if you do not come back—if you do not come back, you will later have regrets even if all turns out well. I also believe it would not feel loving to your wife for you to stay—in spite of Sue's sweet desire to serve the Lord and support you.

He concluded with this directive, "Michael, Get on the plane now! COME HOME NOW, MICHAEL. COME HOME!"

Michael caught the morning flight home the next day. But before he left, he said to me: "I'm so confused, because I'm sure God has called me here, and I know people here need God."

Their baby, born long after our return from the short term, required no surgery as feared. Though Sue was certainly glad to have him back, because she never requested Michael to come home, both feel regret to this day about his return.

I feel deep reservations too. Not about a person leaving a short term to return home—there are times when any missionary, long or short term, needs to return home. Rather, I feel disturbed about the church leader's letter. It displays subtle attitudes toward short-term missions and God's call that we find dangerous to the kingdom.

His e-mail speaks of Sue's "sweet desire to serve the Lord," but doesn't he only mean "misguided" and "naive"? We hear this echoed often in the Christian community. Could it be that the church sees short-term missions as a frivolous endeavor compared to the call of "real life"?

To demand for Michael to come home questions both God's call to Michael and the church's commissioning. Could it be that this echoes the Christian community's idea that short terms are optional, especially if they involve risk, sacrifice or persistence? Could it be that our commissioning services are perfunctory, given more to make people feel good than out of a real sense that God is ordaining a work he has called someone to?

To say it would not *"feel* loving" to Sue if Michael stayed in Guatemala sounds suspiciously as if the church leader elevated feelings of love for family higher than for God. When did a person's life, feelings of love, or family become more important than obedience? Didn't Jesus commend the very thing this man seems to stand against?

> "I tell you the truth," Jesus said to them, "no one who has left home or wife or brothers or parents or children for the sake of the kingdom of God will fail to receive many times as much in this age and, in the age to come, eternal life." (Lk 18:29-30)

Jesus makes no qualifications to this by saying his words are true except with short terms or that things must be okay at home before leaving. Radical? Yes, Jesus' call to follow him is a radical call if one is a missionary or doctor or mailman or housewife.

If the church believes short terms are frivolous, optional programs requiring no risk, major sacrifice or strong sense of call, how could we expect short terms to be anything but superficial? In fact, this is not the problem of "this selfish generation," as we hear so often, but rather the modern church that has forgotten to call us to die for Jesus. Both the church that commissions and those who go need to understand what it means to pick up a cross.

With the mixed messages Michael received, is it any wonder he recently put his call to the missions field on hold and took a position in secular work? He's working as a job recruiter, or headhunter, as it's called in the business world. Can't you see the headlines: "Extra! Read all about it: Would-Be Missionary Becomes Headhunter!"

On the very day Michael sat in the auditorium of Urbana 96 Student Mission Convention, I gathered with the speaking team before Elisabeth Elliot addressed him and eighteen thousand other college students. We split into prayer partners and, as it happened, I was paired with Elisabeth Elliot.

Before praying I said, "Mrs. Elliot, I want you to know that when I was a young Christian, I read your book *Through Gates of Splendor*.[1] I was so profoundly affected by your husband's death on the missions field that when I finished the book, I got down on my knees and committed my life to going wherever God would take me, no matter what."

Mrs. Elliot fixed her steely gaze on me and asked with the verve of a drill sergeant who wanted better, "And where did he take you?"

What a great question! Unimpressed with my *commitment* or her role in it, she wanted to know if it was a commitment kept. Suddenly I realized that I was not talking with a drill sergeant: this woman was a four-star general of the missionary world.

The right answer flashed to my mind: "Lifer with campus ministry, ma'am! Five two-month mission tours in Kenya, two in the Middle East, four in Central America, working on a project in Southeast Asia, ma'am!"

But what I actually croaked out was, "Ministry to college students," and I gave a dumb nod.

She smiled, ever so slightly, and said, "Let's pray."

Her books about her husband Jim Elliot influenced many

more than me. He spent six years working to get the gospel to the Auca people. The tears, the heartaches, the questions all came to a head one day when Jim Elliot and friends met the Auca people on a beach deep in the Ecuadorian jungle.

"On Friday the thrill of Jim's lifetime was given," she writes. "He took an Auca by the hand. At last the twain met. . . . Two days later, on Sunday January 8, 1956, the men for whom Jim Elliot had prayed for six years killed him and his four companions."[2]

Two days of contact for six years of work, leaving behind a wife and nine-month-old daughter? A frivolous, irresponsible use of a life? No doubt, as the front-page headlines of Jim Elliot's death riveted the world, many thought so. But no, he was following Jesus; a life given for Jesus is neither frivolous nor wasted.

When Elisabeth Elliot spoke at Urbana '76 she said that the "will of God is not something you add to your life. It's a course you choose. You either line yourself up with the Son of God and say to the Father, 'Thy will be done,' or you capitulate to the principle which governs the rest of the world and say, 'My will be done.' "[3]

Remember, when Jesus said "Thy will be done," it was in reference to God the Father's will for Jesus to go to the cross—the very place to which he pointed his disciples.

> If anyone would come after me, he must deny himself and take up his cross daily and follow me. For whoever wants to save his life will lose it, but whoever loses his life for me will save it. (Lk 9:23-24)

Anyone means, well, anyone. So do we go on a short term to get something? Yes, go on a short term for what you'll get from it. Just make sure it's not the insipid and puny blessings that so many in the world settle for: to see the world, nice résumé, class credit. Doing missions for those things chokes out the life. Go first to give your life to get life. Then trust God to provide the other stuff as a byproduct of following Jesus with deadly reckless abandon. If you live to protect your life, Jesus says, you lose. But if you lose your life for the sake of Jesus, you find the rich blessings of life. In the end the most radical call is not a missionary call. The most radical call with the greatest blessings comes from living life out of a commitment to the lordship of Christ. That understanding is essential for today's short terms.

7

A God for
All the Potatoes

THERE WOULD BE NO NEED FOR CROSSCULTURAL SKILLS EXCEPT FOR an event years ago, when a group of people got together and said, "Come, let us build ourselves a city, with a tower that reaches to the heavens, so that we may make a name for ourselves and not be scattered over the face of the whole earth." Thus began a building program, spurred on by new technology (mortar) and a new religion (astrology), which attempted to dethrone the living God. God responded to this venture of arrogance by confusing their language and culture. It quickly ended the building project (and corporate apostasy) and became a curse that creates barriers between people to this day.[1] We don't claim to comprehend all the implications of Genesis 11:4, but with each short term we experience the frustration and confusion of Babel.

In fact, after years of short terms we've become experts on babbling. Witness the time when Dave Ivaska ended his rousing missions sermon with the stirring proclamation, in Swahili, that "our God is a God for all nations." Except the word for nations is similar to the word for potatoes, and Dave got them mixed up and proclaimed the somewhat less stirring message that "our God is a God for all the potatoes."

Misunderstanding goes both ways. The word *hello* in Swahili is "jambo." The word for an older respected woman is "mama." You could say hello to the Kenyan president's wife by saying, "Jambo mama," for instance. But this was lost on Janice, a large American woman, who mistakenly took the phrase as "jumbo momma" and thought it a rude reference to her size.

We've been scattered and scattered some more . . .

David Lawrence had hoped that his message for the Guatemalan church would be a rousing story of God's ability to use us in our weakness. Alexa, a student from New York, translated his sermon. David used the passage from 2 Corinthians 4:7: "We have this treasure in jars of clay." As he preached, he noted with satisfaction the mixture of smiles and murmuring coming, no doubt, from his startling insight. He repeated over, with greater vigor, how "we have this treasure in jars of clay." Well, *his* words were okay, but Alexa couldn't quite remember the Spanish word for jars and used urinal instead. After some initial embarrassment David now proudly points out that "urinals for Jesus" has become a euphemism for crosscultural mistakes on our short-term programs.

Other babblings are more serious. President Jimmy Carter was unprepared for the international rift caused by his glib comment about "Montezuma's revenge" during a visit to Mexico. Apparently President Carter was unaware the Mexican people revered Montezuma as a national hero.

From Kosovo to Korea, from America's inner cities to the ethnic strife of central Africa, we see the curse of Babel divide and scatter. Babel is with us today.

> "Come, let us go down and confuse their language so they will not understand each other." So the LORD scattered them from there over all the earth. (Gen 11:7-8)

But there is good news. Though it was God who cursed at Babel, it is also he who redeems. God does not scatter for scattering's sake; his true desire for the nations is to gather. We see that on the day of Pentecost.

> Utterly amazed, they asked: "Are not all these men who are speaking Galileans? Then how is it that each of us hears them in his own native language? Parthians, Medes and Elamites; residents of Mesopotamia, Judea and Cappadocia, Pontus and Asia, Phrygia and Pamphylia, Egypt and the parts of Libya near Cyrene; visitors from Rome (both Jews and converts to Judaism); Cretans and Arabs—we hear them declaring the wonders of God in our own tongues!" (Acts 2:7-11)

At Pentecost we see the most backwater culture (Galileans) speaking the wonders of God in the native languages of most of the world's ethnic groups. It displays God's true heart to gather all tongues and tribes and nations to himself. It was no accident that God displayed his heart at this Jewish celebration of Pentecost. Pentecost *celebrates* harvest! It celebrates gathering in.

Pentecost is a symbol of the redemption God offered from the curse of Babel.[2] It is here that we see God's desire for the nations. The tower of Babel explains why cultures are divided; at Pentecost we see God's true heart to gather all cultures to himself. It points to that day in heaven when all tongues and tribes stand before the throne of God to declare his wonders. At Pentecost, God demonstrated his will on earth just as it is in heaven.

We also see at Pentecost one of the many biblical bases for cultural sensitivity. Note that God did not choose the most widespread language of the day for his miracle, nor did he speak in a heavenly language (as in the Muslim faith). Learning a special language to get to God is not required because God speaks in the common vernacular of everyone on earth.

So when a student from the People's Republic of China asked me, "Does God speak Chinese?" I said confidently, "Yes, he does. God knows your language and culture." God is not a Westerner. He is the Lord of all the earth. God knows all cultures intimately.

God, therefore, is the author of cultural sensitivity. We desire to understand other cultures because *God* knows other cultures. We want to speak in the framework of another person's culture because God spoke in the framework of another's culture. We go to other cultures with the message of redemption as God did rather than requiring other cultures to come to us. We don't ask other cultures to change before they hear the message; rather, we change so that they can hear the message because that's what God did. We want to see things though another culture's eyes because God saw things though our culture's eyes. And on it goes.

If anyone should have understood, it was Peter. He walked with Jesus through the hated Samaritan villages and saw Jesus love them. He heard Jesus declare the temple to be a house of prayer for all nations. Peter stood at the epicenter of Pentecost. God used Peter there to speak the praises of God in other languages. But when it became time for Peter to move out across the gaping divide of cultural differences between Jew and Gentile as a missionary, did Peter get it? Not exactly. When God began working among the Gentiles in Acts 10, Peter's racist attitudes toward Gentiles prohibited him from becoming a (short-term) missionary until God worked on his heart. God started by giving Peter a vision of eating unclean animals.

"Surely not, Lord!" Peter replied (*after* seeing the vision; of course, this is not the first time Peter inappropriately told the Lord what he would or wouldn't do). "I have never eaten anything impure or unclean." The voice spoke to him a second time, "Do not call anything impure that God has made clean" (Acts 10:14-15).

Do not call anything impure God has made clean. Of course, the implication for Peter is not just food; it was people—Gentiles—which Peter called unclean. Before Peter became a missionary, there were some attitudes God needed to change.

For all that Peter saw and did, he remained locked in cultural prejudice after Pentecost. It took continued work on Peter for him to come to grips with how deep his prejudice lay—how deep the curse of Babel had worked its way into Peter's heart.

We're no different. Don't believe you are finished with cultural bias, prejudice and racism just because you have made a commitment to cultural sensitivity or walk with Jesus or live in a more sophisticated society. I wish a single miracle, as on Pentecost, could end once and for all the curse of cultural separation. It didn't for Peter, and it won't for us. Unfortunately, shedding cultural bias and prejudices are some of the hardest things to do in life and won't be solved with a single realization or event. Shedding the lenses of cultural prejudice is better seen as a journey, a journey traveled first by Peter and now by us.

The best place to start this journey is the same place Peter's did: pray. It's not by chance that God's work on Peter's heart happened during Peter's prayer time. We need to ask God to show us our cultural bias before we enter another culture. Name your fears about other cultures to God and examine them in light of God's love for all people. Be open to God's correction in your life. This positions us to move out into other cultures with openness and to recognize that some of the people we may least expect to follow God will do so.

*   *   *

The directions the missionaries gave me for their home in the Masai Mara of the Rift Valley went something like this: "At this point, you'll leave the pavement for a number of miles—travel down this dirt road till you come to a tree—you can't miss it, it's the only one. Turn east on the riverbed. (Don't worry, it hasn't rained for a couple of years now.) *Don't miss this turn*—if you do, you'll go to Tanzania. Follow the riverbed a couple of hours till you come to the first village, just stop in the village and ask for us. We'll be waiting for you." *A couple of hours?* Did that mean two or more?

If the rental car agency in downtown Nairobi knew where I planned on taking their Fiat Uno, they would have never rented me the car.

I dropped off two wide-eyed students, Scott and David, who were to live with the missionaries for three weeks. I said good-bye, and they responded with limp waves and forlorn looks that pulled at my heart as they grew smaller in my rearview mirror. But no matter, I knew they were in good hands. They would feel at home in a matter of days. And besides, my adventure down the riverbed in the middle of the Masai Mara so excited me that it was hard to feel sorry for anyone. The sandy riverbed made for a surprisingly smooth ride, and since I no longer felt concern about accidentally driving to Tanzania, I took in the view. Giraffes crossed my path walking their gangly walk. Ostriches ran up beside me on the bank and then scattered. A stealthy big cat on the prowl streaked away as he saw the yellow Uno come his way. On occasion, I saw a Masai warrior. Masai are the statuesque people of the Serengeti plains of East Africa. They cut and stretch their ear lobes into long hoops, which they decorate with beads. They wear colorful blankets. They carry long spears to protect their cattle from lions. They love cattle. As I rounded a wide bend in the riverbed, I came upon two warriors standing on one leg in stork fashion leaning on their spears. They motioned to me for a ride.

What the heck, I thought.

These two guys thought *I* looked exotic. After all, a white guy driving a Fiat Uno down riverbeds, dressed in a polo shirt, may have been the oddest thing they had ever seen. They stared and laughed at me. I smiled back. They weren't that familiar with cars (they puzzled over the door handles). We started as soon as they got settled: one spear trailed out the right back window, one spear trailed out the left back window. We looked like some strange insect buzzing across the sand.

Though unfamiliar with Fiat door handles, they immediately recognized the radio and motioned for me to turn it on. I was in the middle of the Rift Valley in East Africa and quite sure we were out of range of any radio station. But to humor them I turned it on and began scanning the band. Sure enough, only static came from the speakers. I almost switched it off when—blip—I heard the brief sound of a station. I backtracked, and to my surprise, a channel came in loud and clear.

It was . . . it was Dolly Parton and Kenny Rogers singing "Islands in the Stream." And the Masai guys *loved* it. They were slapping their bare knees to keep time with the music. You would have thought they had grown up in Nashville, not Narok.

Well, one bridge was built over a chasm of cultural differences. I decided to try out my Masai.

"Sopa," I said.

"Epa," they responded with raised eyebrows, surprised that I knew the language.

"Ai supati enkeria?" I asked.

"A, ai supat enkeria!" They said with genuine shock that I would know more.

"Ai supati enkeshu?" I asked.

"A, ai supat enkeshu!" they responded laughing. Now it was their turn to be surprised. It sounded like babbling to me, but it had their attention.

"Ne na ku talilo," I said.

"Ne na ku talilo!" they responded, grinning to each other.

I was giving the ritual greetings for Masai, having asked, roughly, "How are the children and how are the cows?" (Masai can greet each other for hours), and then said "and that's the way it goes." They began telling me all about the cows and the children. Unfortunately, I had exhausted my Masai, but I knew one more phrase.

"Messisi Enkai." I announced while I pointed to myself and then to the sky.

"Messisi Enkai!" they shouted. "A, messisi Enkai!"

"Messisi Yesu?" they asked.

"A!" I exclaimed, "Messisi Yesu!"

They began thumping me on the back and hugging me. I had just given a greeting that Masai Christians gave to one another, and they responded with joy. These Masai warriors were brothers in Christ.

I babbled, "Messisi Enkai! Messisi Yesu!"—"Praise God, Praise Jesus," I was praising the wonders of God in another language and almost ran that Fiat Uno into the bank of the riverbed.

Praise God! Praise Jesus! A white guy in a polo shirt from Kentucky, and two Masai warriors from Kenya together in a Fiat Uno on a dry riverbed in the Masai Mara worshiping God together! What joy! I hadn't seen it coming. I suppose I was locked into what I thought Masai were supposed to be. But there it was: some of the sweetest fellowship I have ever known. I knew the redemption of Babel.

It's one of the greatest joys of a short-term mission—seeing God break down barriers that separate us. We get to taste what heaven will be like—to know hints of the joy of Pentecost, to glimpse our gathering before the throne of God.

8

Kenyan House-Help

IF WE CONTINUE OUR READING OF ACTS 10, WE SEE THAT PETER DID something most Jewish men didn't do—he visited the house of a Gentile, Cornelius. And since his trip to the Gentile's home in Caesarea lasted about four days, he had led the first New Testament short-term missions trip.

Cornelius, when he met Peter, "fell at his feet in reverence. But Peter made him get up. 'Stand up,' he said, 'I am only a man myself' " (Acts 10:25-26).

Peter does not allow Cornelius to worship him, nor does Peter treat Cornelius as unclean. Peter explains what he knows of why he is there.

> You are well aware that it is against our law for a Jew to associate
> with a Gentile or visit him. But God has shown me that I should

not call any man impure or unclean. So when I was sent for, I came without raising any objection. May I ask why you sent for me? (Acts 10:28-29)

Peter makes for a wonderful example of how to enter a new culture.

Peter learned from God what is clean and unclean. Be careful about letting your culture dictate what is clean and unclean. Usually, our preferences and tastes are not biblical but cultural. Don't give up because you encounter something hard in another culture; wonder about it as Peter did. Maybe it's how people interact, perhaps it's thinking of certain practices as unclean as it was for Peter. Maybe it's a challenge to how you think things should be done. Ask what bigger lesson God has for you.

Peter entered the Gentile culture with humility and a desire to serve. "I am only a man myself," Peter said. Are we willing to say along with Peter that I am just a person myself? Can we put aside the adulation that some are quick to heap on us in another culture, adulation that mimics worship? Are we willing to put aside our natural desires to be served? The temptation to be served is strong when in another culture.

How we use our money, our education and our know-how provide a powerful temptation to sidestep the hard work of servanthood. Once we've given ourselves over to the temptation to be powerful, we get Peter's model with Cornelius backwards: we become master and teacher rather than servant and learner. We become people who quickly jump in to teach, correct and direct before we ever earn the right to do so.

Peter did not enter with all the answers. Anyone who has studied the life of Peter knows this is a major change for him. Rather, Peter displays a willingness to ask questions of how God has spoken to them.

Are we humble enough to learn from our hosts? Or do we arrive at the home of our hosts with a set idea of what we are to teach? Can we trust that God has been at work before the plane landed? Or do we think that we are the only ones who hear God's voice?

Too many short-term missions focus on task rather than life in Christ. Too many short-term missions are focused on an agenda and not enough on what God may have for us. We don't mean to excuse sloppy, mismanaged short terms run by lazy directors. We're simply calling for a willingness to follow Peter's example of working on attitude before task.

One year in Guatemala, our work project was to tear down a building another short-term program had built. When we asked the purpose of the building Manuel smiled and said, "Last year a group came, and they told us that God wanted them to build a building for us. We didn't need a building, but they didn't ask, and we didn't want them to feel bad, so we let them build that building you are now tearing down."

Don't forget to ask, along with Peter, "Why am I here?" Don't forget to serve.

Kenyan House-Help

An elderly African gentleman spoke to us during our orientation in Kenya. We sat in a circle around him. His soft, lilting African-English echoed in the concrete room. Though his words fell gently on our ears, they pierced my heart.

"Bwana Asafiwe" (Praise the Lord), he said. "I love the Lord Jesus with all my heart." This is a greeting we heard often from Christians in Kenya. He said he felt nervous but honored to speak to an American group. "My parents came to Christ through missionaries from your country," he said. "The missionaries buried two of their children here. I am grateful to them for their sacrifice. I am grateful to your country for sending them." We felt tinges of pride.

Then, almost apologetically, he said, "Today, my young brothers and sisters, I fear for you." He used the podium to steady himself. "Your great strength is now your weakness. Many no longer know how to share as Jesus did, with humility, like a servant."

It's hard to tell what students heard, but I don't think he had an impact. We don't want to hear things like that. We want to believe we're different. Besides, the old man was only one of many speakers, and we kept the students busy. We spent the rest of the week studying the book of Philippians and preparing for specific assignments.

At the end of orientation, we scattered students across Kenya to live in African-Christian homes. Joanne went to live with the Ndutiris.

Mr. Ndutiri worked for a youth ministry to high school kids. Stories circulated during orientation about revival among Kenyan students. "Joanne, get ready to reap a harvest," one orientation visitor told her.

"High school kids come to Christ in droves at every meeting," another said.

This talk excited Joanne. Joanne became a Christian through the ministry of Young Life in high school. She worked as a Young Life leader in college. This assignment had the feel of a perfect fit. She polished her testimony. She worked on a sermon. She looked forward to ushering in God's kingdom through her evangelistic efforts.

The Ndutiri's home was a typical African city home. They had running water and electricity, unlike many places other students stayed. But they faced their share of hardships too. Joanne arrived during Mrs. Ndutiri's ninth month of pregnancy. Mrs. Ndutiri struggled to do the housework.

We oriented Kenyan families for their American guests with our motto: "Our students come as servants and learners. Treat them as family, not as guests. Put them to work in what would best serve Christ." The Ndutiris took us literally. They asked Joanne to do the housework.

Housework is hard in Kenya. Joanne said later that she didn't know much about housework in America, much less in Kenya. Imagine doing an entire family's wash by hand. Joanne bargained at the open market for food. She scrubbed floors, laundry and kids. Joanne cleaned and cooked chicken (Mr. Ndutiri slaughtered the chicken, though he puzzled over Joanne's squeamishness). She served the meals and did the dishes. She served tea, a Kenyan custom, twice a day. Guests, another Kenyan custom, streamed in for breakfast, lunch and dinner. Joanne fell in bed each evening exhausted from fumbling through foreign routines in a foreign land.

Initially Joanne bided her time until the real ministry of evangelism started. Her first thoughts sounded more reasonable than angry. First angry thoughts always do. *I've raised a lot of money. I've come a long way. I sure hope we get to do something useful.*

The Ndutiris didn't say please and thank you either. The Ndutiris appreciated Joanne. She was a Godsend for them. But Kenyans show their appreciation in ways other than saying please and thank you. These words are rarely used in Swahili. Joanne didn't know that. To her, they sounded rude. "Joanne, fix the tea. Joanne, do the wash. Joanne, change the babies."

I'm getting a degree in nursing, thought Joanne. *Surely there is something I could do better than this.*

During the second week Joanne wondered why they hadn't gone to the high schools. At first, Joanne thought Mr. Ndutiri was dragging his feet. No, Mr. Ndutiri just canceled all their engagements—the baby was due any day, and there was too much to do at the house for Joanne to talk to high-school students. Dread fell on Joanne: three weeks . . . at the Ndutiris . . . as the house-help.

What will my supporters think when I tell them all I did on my short-term mission was clean house? wondered Joanne.

As Joanne's dreams for high school evangelism fizzled, she wondered about other student's exciting adventures. She envisioned their glorious opportunities. She felt ripped off.

Toward the end of her second week, as she was hanging the wash on the line, she had had enough. The crushing responsibilities of a home plus the added weight of another culture boiled over.

"I'm here as a guest in their home, and how do they treat me?" she said. "I'm better than this," she said. She stomped her foot. "Why, they're treating me like I'm the help. They just want me to be their . . . their servant."

And then it hit her—right there in an African backyard between a banana tree and the clothesline. "What was it that old man said at orientation?" The full force of Joanne's study in the book of Philippians punched through.

> Your attitude should be the same as that of Christ Jesus: Who, being in very nature God, did not consider equality with God something to be grasped, but made himself nothing, taking the very nature of a *servant*. (Phil 2:5-7, my emphasis)

There it was, as clear and bright as the African sky. To hang the Ndutiri's wash was to be like Jesus.

The work around the house didn't change. If anything, it was more difficult since Mrs. Ndutiri gave birth to their third child during Joanne's last week. But Joanne changed. The baby was a joy, and Joanne was now a part of the family. She finished her time with the Ndutiris with little fanfare. Joanne never became a great Kenyan evangelist, though she did make it to a couple of high schools. More important than the projects she did was her witness of servanthood.

A week later Shiro met some friends on the streets of Nairobi. Shiro, a Kenyan student, took part in our program with Joanne. Her friends confronted her, "What are you doing with all these Americans?"

"Oh, no," said Shiro. "They're not like the others. Some of these people served as house-help in Kenyan homes." Her friends looked flabbergasted.

The word rang out. African Christians looked at our group differently. We soon explored partnerships between Kenyan university students and our group.

The following summer Kenyan and American students joined each other for a week-long evangelistic outreach. We journeyed to Masai country on the edge of the Rift Valley. The outreach was the most powerful evangelistic effort I've ever known. Hundreds of people came to Christ due, in part, to the witness of American and Kenyan Christian students working together.

One night during our outreach, I slipped out of my sleeping bag and took a walk under the African stars. I wondered if our outreach would have happened without Joanne. It wasn't her power that served as a witness but her humility. Joanne *did* usher in God's kingdom, though it happened in a way she didn't expect. She didn't even get to see it.

I thought about stars in the Bible:

Do everything without complaining or arguing, so that you may become blameless and pure, children of God without fault in a crooked and depraved generation, in which you shine like stars in the universe as you hold out the word of life. (Phil 2:14-16)

Stars in the universe. The same stars Abraham counted in the desert. Of all the powerful programs and projects we did in Africa, from hunger relief to hut-to-hut evangelism, from working in clinics to preaching to high-school youth groups, none made us more available to non-Christians as an American house helper in a Kenyan home.

Joanne didn't even get to see the outreach, but she saw the point. She offered herself as a humble servant. It came with struggle, but what important thing doesn't? In the mix Joanne grew more like Jesus. That's worth the trip—I'd bet even Joanne's supporters thought so.[1]

9

Questions of Trust

ONE SUMMER BRIAN AND I TRAVELED TO A MUSLIM COUNTRY FOR our program there. We placed the students with Muslim families and had good contact with the university, but Brian's housing had not worked out as planned for his family. The dean of the university met with us during the first week to review how things were going. Brian shared how the students seemed to be having a great time with their host families and the program was going very well, but there was just one glitch: his family needed housing. They couldn't stay in a dorm room with no kitchen. The dean, with a flourish of his hand stated grandly, "Well, that's no problem. You can use my summer cottage not far from here." Brian and I looked at each other, scarcely believing our great fortune, then we looked back at the dean and said, "Well, thank you very much, Dean. We really appreciate it." The dean looked a bit flustered, but we moved on to other topics. We left his office rejoicing that the dean had taken care of Brian's needs.

But complications kept preventing Brian's move (the summer cottage was too dirty one week, some construction was needed the next). Day after day, as Brian pressed the dean about his offer, it became clear the dean had no intention of Brian and his family moving into the summer cottage. Brian began to feel that the dean wasn't being straight with him and wondered why the dean acted as if he were being rude.

After all, wasn't it lying to offer something with no intention to do it? Perhaps, and certainly in our culture. But Brian and I simply hadn't followed the proper pattern of communication. In the Middle East one doesn't do things so directly. If we had followed proper protocol, the conversation should have gone much more like this:

"You can use my summer cottage."

"Oh no, Dean we could never impose upon you like that."

"No, I insist that you stay in my summer cottage, despite the fact that my wife and I spend our vacation time there."

"Oh, thank you, Dean, but we will try hard to find another place to stay."

"Well, if you must you must, but please know that I am concerned for you."

No, the dean wasn't lying. He was only doing what would have been well understood in the Middle East. In the West, perhaps, it would have been a gracious offer; in Middle-Eastern culture it was a show of concern.[1] But because Brian and the dean did not understand each other, it undermined their trust of each other.

For years we have taught short termers to ask the prior question of trust,[2] or PQT. It's asked this way: "Is what I'm thinking, saying and doing building or undermining trust?" Ask this question in any and all crosscultural settings.[3] The prior question of trust is a helpful tool to take out those cultural obstacles hindering the gospel. Remember it this way: no matter how interesting your story, spinach between teeth distracts from what you say. Spinach between your teeth is not immoral, but it's hard to listen to someone when it happens. In the same way, cultural ignorance distracts from the message of Christ.

The process of asking the prior question of trust helps us follow Paul's principle to "become all things to all men so that by all possible means I might save some" (1 Cor 9:22).

We're going to list twelve basic nonmoral issues in every culture that can build or demolish trust. See how asking the prior question of trust in these situations can serve to break down barriers to crosscultural communication.

Language

Nothing establishes trust like speaking the language. You may feel like you're babbling, but as Thomas and Elizabeth Brewster say, language learning *is* ministry.[4] It's enough to just try. The trust that is built by saying "I'm willing to look stupid in your language" is worth a thousand mistakes about potatoes and urinals. Take a stab at the language.

We enroll our short termers in language schools for a brief time on their trips so that they can take those first steps. We've also enrolled our children in Spanish immersion schools in the city where we live because we have come to understand how much knowing another language opens up the world—not to mention how helpful they are to translate for their parents when we take a short-term trip in a Spanish-speaking country.

Food

Stab at the food too. Besides the fact that it may be alive, food is an important part of understanding and appreciating culture.

John knew Japanese desserts were not sweet as American desserts, so he was not surprised when the cookie he was served along with his tea did not taste as good as it looked. The Japanese hosts smiled and nodded, a young child pointed, and John felt glad he was jumping into Japanese culture so smoothly as he munched on his cookie—that is, until cleanup. That's when he noticed his polite hosts gathering cork coasters and stacking them in a coaster rack—all but the one he had eaten.

That's okay. At least he tried. It's no wonder that God used food in the vision to help Peter shed his prejudice toward other cultures. God still uses food to help us understand. A great way to establish trust is to be able to enjoy the food of other cultures.

"Mack, I'm sorry," said Jeb. "I know they call this food here, but back home we call this bait."

Yes, food can be difficult, but show some enthusiasm for trying. Sometimes the greatest problem to overcome is attitude, not taste buds. It was amazing how quickly Jeb sincerely learned to like the seafood in China.

Learn local staples before you arrive and ask for them. Eat the food and eat it the way it's eaten there. If it's with a fork, use a fork; if it's chopsticks, use chopsticks; if it's with your hand, learn to use your hand.

Dress

We need to know how to dress in our target culture. All cultures have "rules" of appropriateness for dress in given situations, the nuances of which are never clear to an outsider. In many Western countries the way we choose to dress is seen as a freedom or an expression of our individuality. Many cultures, however, do not share our concern for self-expression. For many, the ways of dress are set, and deviations are seen as an indication of low character. So to establish trust, be careful to know how to dress, and plan your wardrobe accordingly.

It's not just what clothes to put on, it has to do with how we dress too. In some parts of Kenya women don't show their knees in public; when Leeann hiked up her dress to exit the backs of *matatus* (public transports that are basically pickup trucks with seats in the back), she exposed herself indecently by their standards. It was shocking and accounted for the stares she got from the women around her. Did she mean to offend? Of course not, but it broke trust with the Kenyans.

Be sensitive about traditional dress and Christian dress too. In some cultures a foreigner who dons traditional dress may be received warmly; in other cultures it may be seen as presumptuous. After forming relationships with national people, ask if it would be appropriate for you to wear a traditional outfit and then do it under their guidance.

By "Christian" dress we don't mean prudish stereotypes. Rather, we want to submit ourselves to national believers and their understanding. For example, make-up and certain kinds of jewelry in some cultures are associated with witchcraft, pagan worship or prostitution. In the Middle East many Christian symbols are associated with the Crusades.

Gender Issues

It was a hot summer day in North Africa—it's *always* hot on summer days in North Africa. So when Leeann, Shannon and our three boys walked to the market in town and spied an ice-cream stand, they couldn't resist. They settled down to enjoy their cones under a big tree in the park across the street. But a hazy awareness came over them that something wasn't right.

Suddenly Shannon jumped up, grabbed Leeann's arm and whispered, "Let's get out of here!" When they were safely down the street a bit, Shannon giggled, "Leeann, we were the only two women in that whole park! Did you see how they were staring at us?" As we came to understand the culture a little better, we learned that men and women tend to spend their time separated: women gather in homes and men in the public places.

Gender norms are different the world around. It is not unusual for women to be seated on one side of a room and men on the other in church—or to find only men in the park. Don't assume that interactions between men and women will be same as what you are used to. You'll need to observe carefully. Ask open-ended questions in order to understand what is acceptable. Don't ask, "Your culture wouldn't be so stupid as to believe that a simple hug means she's a loose woman, would it?" Ask, "What do most people in this culture think when they see two people hug on the street?"

Remember too that the cultural rules apply to how you relate with your fellow team members as well as nationals. What may be a no big deal hug between two friends in some cultures communicates open prostitution in another. Again, this is not a lesson in prudishness; it's a lesson about becoming all things to all people so that we can speak the gospel without putting anything in the way of it being heard. It establishes trust.

Cultural Communication Patterns

When we cross a culture, we need to be prepared for communication to follow very different patterns from ours. This is where Brian and I struggled with the dean of the university. These patterns are never obvious, but being aware that communication patterns are different along with good observation will help build trust.

Western culture tends to communicate directly:

$$A \rightarrow B$$

African and Middle-Eastern culture spirals toward the subject:

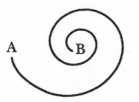

Asian culture circles the subject:

Time Views

Great frustrations build when a person from a culture that marches to the tick of a clock encounters another with a completely different rhythm. One person comes off as rude and brusque, the other as inefficient and wasteful. We can be unnerved by the way people deal with time. Consider longer church services. To some it seems as if the leaders are wasting time, while to others it's clear they are not paying enough attention to the here and now.

Leeann quickly learned that most Kenyans are not very time conscious. Meetings began late, services went on for hours and people didn't necessarily come to visit us when they said they would. So the second trip she decided to leave her watch at home. She reasoned that if she didn't have a watch, she wouldn't worry about the time. After driving me crazy with two months asking the time, she realized her view of time would not be changed by losing her watch.

Leeann's view changed when she came to appreciate the emphasis in their culture on the person. She needed to see that

Kenyans celebrate their visitors. They give them warm greetings, special services and their time. Remember, as visitors to another culture, we need to adjust to their orientation to time and not superimpose our own.

Respect

In our culture, respect is something that needs to be earned. It is something that can be won or lost. Honoring someone simply because they have lived a long time seems simplistic. But in many cultures, respect is something that is given automatically according to some status such as age or position. Most of the world reveres older people and feel youth have simply not earned the right to speak about much of anything.

As a young mother with a five-month-old baby, Leeann faced a dilemma. When we traveled with Tristan to the Masai village, the women found him to be a fascinating novelty and longed to hold this blond baby. Their curiosity often so overcame their hospitality they would tear him out of her arms. Trying to get him from each other was even more forceful, almost violent. The sound of Tristan's desperate cries and arms stretched out for her while the women of the village fought to hold him still wrenches her heart today. Back then it just scared her, but she knew she needed to find the right solution to avoid burning bridges with the people of the village. So one day, before the women mobbed us, she spied out the oldest woman in the village and placed Tristan in her arms. A number of things happened almost immediately. First, and most notable, Tristan stopped crying—that woman knew a thing or two about babies. Second, almost as quickly, the younger women sat down around the elder woman to wait their turn. And finally, Leeann built trust because she had shown the proper respect.

Frame of Reference

Frame of reference is simply what you know about your world. If you speak out of your frame of reference with no regard for someone else's frame of reference, you won't establish trust.

Two summers ago in Guatemala, one of our students was asked to give his testimony in a small village church. Matt started his story like this:

> I'm a college student at UM, and I'm on the tennis team. Before the season started, our team had a hot-dog roast on the beach, and Coach and I got to talking about . . .

And on it went. His audience listened politely, but they didn't understand a word he said. Their village didn't even have a grade school, so they certainly didn't understand "college" or what a "UM" was. And in a village without a teacher, they certainly didn't know about a coach. They had never seen a tennis court, tennis ball, tennis racket or tennis team. Their dogs were the four-legged kind, and the idea of roasting one seemed very uncivilized. Since they had never seen the ocean, they didn't have any idea what a beach was . . . You get the picture: it's a frame of reference.

When speaking to a person of a different culture, we need to understand how his or her frame of reference differs from ours. Start by stripping idiomatic phrases out of your speech. Establish points of common understanding: things such as children, fears, loves, God.

Humor

Humor often is a source of building or breaking trust. Humor in a new culture frequently sounds negative. This is especially true for laughter you hear from a group or laughter you make as a group.

When Greg Jobe tripped and fell, his Kenyan friends laughed. Greg felt made fun of and offended. But later, when he talked with another Kenyan friend, he discovered that was the way people dealt with awkward situations. They were laughing to help minimize his embarrassment.

Gift Giving

In some cultures, arriving without a gift is inexcusable. How to receive gifts and how to give gifts can be ruled by protocol unknown unless we ask. Sometimes we must be careful who we give gifts to. The gift I gave to Ngarachu's daughter was not inappropriate (a small McDonald's happy-meal figure), but she has fifteen brothers and sisters. I should have given the gift to her father and let him figure out which child would play with it.

Money

We have seen many in the West feel that the best thing they can do in a situation is give money. But often giving large sums of money to very poor people can be the most damaging thing to do. Please be generous, but discover the way locals give. If you don't know how locals give, you should wait till you do.

Understanding Moral Issues

By definition we are dealing with nonmoral issues. There are some aspects of culture that the Christian must always stand against, regardless of its roots in the culture. Child sacrifice or slavery, for example. This sets the missionary apart from the cultural anthropologist (who maintains a commitment to never change another's culture).[5] Yet we must be careful when we deal with moral issues too. Sometimes moral issues can be approached from very different perspectives.

Nearly all cultures believe stealing is bad. But while most cultures see hopping a fence and taking something out of a yard as stealing, for some Native-American groups, erecting a fence is stealing. Eating beef in some parts of India, exposing a woman's triceps in some parts of Korea, using your left hand in parts of the Middle East are all moral issues we might miss. Learn about these practices to establish trust.

It goes the other way. There are cultural mores we hold strongly that are not regarded as important by other cultures. Jill felt betrayed that Fatima read her journal. Fatima simply did not see a problem with using, reading and involving herself with Jill's stuff. Some cultures feel that anything written in their home is communal property. Though we had specifically said during orientation that this culture would view most everything as communal property, Jill decided that the people of that culture were immoral and trust was broken.

There are many issues that can make or break trust. Making sure to ask yourself the prior question of trust (it doesn't hurt to memorize it), coupled with the ability to distinguish between nonmoral issues, goes a long way toward a graceful bridge into another culture. Our next chapter deals with the inevitable shock when we actually make the move into another culture.

10

Culture Shock!

CROSSING CULTURES IS FLAT-OUT FUN FOR MACK. HE SAYS HE SEES God in the diversity of the world. Crossing cultures is more difficult for me. I tend to see God in the things that don't change—after all, immutability is part of God's character too. Unlike Mack, I know I'm not crossing a culture for the thrill of crossing the culture. My lessons come harder, but I like to think they go deeper.

Living in Kenya felt different enough, but Masai culture made me feel downright alien. Jesus commanded, "Go ye therefore to the uttermost," and boy, did I feel I had found the land of utter. One Sunday, early during our first trip, we visited a Masai village for church. It was a lengthy service, but finally the women of the church gave one last song—a robust hymn of praise to Jesus sung in *Ma*[1] with a traditional Masai tune. While the women sang, they swayed their long earlobes, decorated with beads and earrings, back and forward in time to the music. Then church ended, five hours after it started—five hours of sitting on a rough plank that rocked unsteadily on cinder blocks, five hours of brushing flies off my squirming baby. I walked stiffly toward the door, letting a bony dog exit first. Men talked on the wood front porch, much as men do everywhere after church, except as they talked, they sorted through the various spears and clubs left at the door, knowing it improper to be armed in church. As they looked at the sky, I imagined their talk concerned the coming rains. A tap tapping on the tin roof of the church signaled the arrival of the rainy season. I watched the miniature explosions of red dust on the ground, *piff* . . . *piff* . . . *piff*, as the rain hit.

Masai men's earlobes are cut too and stretched long enough to hook over the top of their ear. The quick motion they use always reminds me of a woman tucking her hair behind her ear. As the men stepped out from under the shelter of the roof, some tucked their lobes over the tops of their ears as they ran for cover. Others popped umbrellas and began their long trek home—some had hours to walk. I enjoyed the odd incongruity of Masai herdsman carrying their British umbrellas. I felt ready to go home too.

But a family in the village invited us to their home and Mack and our Masai friend Philip Kishoyian quickly accepted. Their home sat on a piece of ground about 100 feet in diameter. There were no roads, no electricity, no phone, no running water. Dirt paths crisscrossed their way from home to home, but the actual homes were difficult to see, since the owners hemmed in their dwelling with a "fence" made of briars and bushes.

"To keep the lions out," the owner told me and then, catching a hint of fear in my eyes, added, "but the lions stay far over there." He pointed to a hill in the distance. I knew he said this to reassure me, but any uncaged lions seemed too close to me. "Oh," I said.

The fence also kept the cows *in*. They wandered about the property. Of course, this was the source of flies that covered Tristan's face. They seemed to go for his eyes. "Leeann," Philip whispered, "don't brush them away. They think it's rude."

"Oh," I said.

We ducked low to enter into the house that looked like a brown igloo. The Masai make their homes from the cakes of cow manure. I tried to keep a positive cultural mindset while trying to avoid rubbing against the wall, but it proved to be a difficult tension. To make matters worse, women in the hut snatched Tristan out of my arms and began passing him around. I wanted to be culturally sensitive, but the women seemed to be spitting on him. Later I discovered that this was a ritual for babies in Masai culture—to treat them as if they are ugly helps them avoid the attention of demons—but at the time all I could think about was the Centers for Disease Control and Prevention warnings that tuberculosis is endemic in Masai culture. He whimpered and held out his arms to me . . . I bit my lip. I felt confused.

At first, in the darkness all I could see was the fire on the floor in the middle of the small room, but my eyes adjusted, and I looked around. The dirt floor was cracked but amazingly smooth, almost polished from years of wear. A calendar picture of a Wisconsin snow scene hung on the wall, years out of date and worlds out of place. The best thing about the inside of the dung hut was that there were no flies—no flies because the smoke from the fire filled the room. My eyes watered and Tristan coughed. I worried about his asthma. I could not have felt more out of place if you had put me on Mars.

Mack and Philip talked with an elder, one of the first Masai to come to Christ in that district. I was not invited into that discussion since I was to be with the women, but they spoke no English. Simply knowing that the Masai culture was patriarchal didn't help. I felt misunderstood. After all, I *was* the codirector of the Kenyan program. To make matters worse, Mack seemed to be having a great time, which irritated me all the more. He acted as if he we were casually stopping by a friend's house for lunch after church. Actually, that's exactly what had happened, and lunch became the final straw.

The Masai staple is a drink they call sour milk: milk left in charred gourds and allowed to curdle. It tastes a bit like buttermilk, except it's lumpy, and sometimes they mix cow urine or cow blood with it. Embarrassed, I stared at the beat-up tin measuring cup containing what I knew to be a generous offer. I wanted to be open. I just couldn't choke it down. Watching Mack drink his second helping with gusto increased my nausea and frustration. Tristan started to cry. I couldn't see him very well because of the smoke, and that's when I hit the wall: I couldn't do it anymore. I stumbled across the room and grabbed Tristan. I pressed him tight to me. I twirled around, gave my cup to Mack and hissed, "You drink it." Mack gave me his what's-got-into-you look. No time to explain. I made a beeline for the door, crawled though it awkwardly in my culturally sensitive skirt and ran past the hedge fence (slipping and sliding on cow pies) to a dirt trail. I'd show those Masai who could walk—I headed home, not Ngong or Nairobi. Home. Never mind that I wasn't quite sure how to get there, never mind the lions or the Sahara and a couple of oceans. I marched west.

But on my trek back to America, I found myself passing the church. It was empty, so I crept inside and sat once more on a rough wood plank to change a messy diaper and to have a good cry—under the watchful stare of about twenty kids who followed me down the road.

Culture shock is that realization of how inadequately your world fits with their world. We experience bits of culture shock all along life's road. Marriage is an adjustment because two people's family cultures collide. Job changes are stressful because corporate cultures are different. Many people feel the clash of culture when they go to a new church. All of these can produce various levels of culture shock. But for the most part we cope with these different cultures almost imperceptibly and in ways that are understood by those around us.

But when it hits crossculturally, the differences are so strong that they overwhelm our normal coping mechanisms. You can't talk it through because they don't speak your language. They don't understand why you don't like to eat it; they eat it every day. Explaining how you do it in America only comes off as a putdown of their culture. Culture shock is the stunning emotions that accompany our move into a different world, usually (but not always) negative.

Peter felt culture shock over food, just like me. The request, from God no less, left him aghast. Peter felt shock about being with people whom he had been told were unclean. (Peter's companions were stunned by the Gentiles response to the gospel too—a positive but no less disorienting emotion). I'm tempted to see Peter's understanding of people as provincial, that is until I notice the similarities between him and my feelings about the Masai women passing around my baby.

I know now that what I felt in that Masai hut was inevitable. To cross a culture without experiencing some culture shock is to become a tourist who observes and enjoys the culture as a mere spectator. More comfortable, perhaps, but ultimately isolated from the culture.

Many short termers feel that the goal is to avoid the feelings of culture shock. Some go lengths to avoid it, and some feel they fail if they struggle. Some directors set up their programs to avoid culture shock altogether. But this is simply a misunderstanding of a process. If you truly cross a culture, you will feel culture shock. Today if a short termer says he or she felt no culture shock on our short term, we feel like apologizing.

Not that I was wishing for more culture shock while I sat in that Masai church. Usually when you're in culture shock, you're not worried about understanding it. The mixture of emotions I felt in that hut—confusion, frustration, embarrassment and even repulsion—seemed too overwhelming.

It was not enough that I felt called of God. It was not enough that I had a biblical mindset. It was not enough that I wanted with all my heart to be a servant to the Masai people. The stronger the culture shock, the more likely various differences are hitting you at once. And when they do, there are some things you can remember.

First, take heart: culture shock means you are entering a different culture. Jesus entered into our world in a building not that different than a Masai hut, and he came from a culture much nicer than America; he came from the culture of heaven.

Next, remember that culture shock comes to us for many different reasons, in different places, at different times—many of those reasons we listed in chapter nine. Remember, too, you are not weird because you feel intense culture shock even when others don't. Living conditions pose little problem for Mack (something I attribute to the way he kept his college apartment), so Masai huts were not a problem. But dealing with embarrassment or loss of face crossculturally is a very different matter for him.

Know too that we rarely see culture shock coming. Those places where we least expect to feel culture shock are the places we sometimes feel it the greatest. The Canadians on our Guatemala program, for instance, felt the greatest culture shock not with the Guatemalans but with their American teammates.

When I fled the Masai hut, though no one said anything to me (it had barely been noticed), I thought I had blown it, that I would never be able to cross a culture with the gospel. Now I see it is not the feelings that are bad—I felt what most people in my situation would have felt—the potential for bad was how I responded to my feelings.

Over time I came to love visiting the Masai. After working though my experience of culture shock, I went back to that small village. I learned to sit in a Masai hut, pass around my kids and drink sour milk with the best of them. Best of all, I could see love in these people, love rarely seen in the West—I was learning from them. Coping with culture shock brings powerful rewards.

What to do? Start by not worrying about it. Jump in. No one crosses a culture without feeling culture shock. It may come at different times in different ways for different reasons, but rest assured it will happen. You can count on that (that and the fact it will probably be inconvenient).

And when it does, know how to cope with culture shock; the subject of the next chapter.

11

Redlining

WE ALL WILL HIT CULTURE SHOCK. THE VARIABLE IS HOW WE RESPOND.
Do we push though culture shock into understanding and rapport, or do we become critical, defensive and isolate ourselves? The response carries much weight for how our message will be heard in that culture.

By all appearances Sarah seemed a strong candidate for our short term. A student from New Jersey, Sarah came from a missions-minded church. She was a leader in her Christian fellowship group on campus. She had known that she wanted to be a missionary since she was a little girl. Sarah felt called to the Muslim world. By her application alone, Sarah was a sure thing.

But applications are not real life. When Sarah hit the inevitable culture shock, rather than working though it, Sarah chose to *redline:* the word we use for isolating ourselves from the culture. Isolation takes different forms; for Sarah it was her Sony Walkman—but I'm getting ahead of the story.

Twenty students took part in our pilot program to the Middle East. When we stepped off the plane in the capital city, we discovered both how hot the Middle East gets in the summer and the warmth of Arab hospitality. Far from the nasty American stereotypes about Arabs being terrorists, we found our hosts to be some of the most gracious and welcoming people we had ever met. And Sohalia was the most gracious of the group.

Sohalia, highly relational and sweet-spirited, went to great lengths to welcome her guest Sarah. When Sohalia met Sarah, she took Sarah's hands in hers, looked her in the eye and said, "Oh, I do hope you like my country."

Sohalia later told me how all her life she had wanted an American friend, "That's why I'm an English major," she said.

Before Sohalia's family drove off with Sarah to their home, Sohalia assured me that she would get to see a wonderful and beautiful side of life in her country.

Sohalia wasn't just a warm host; she had the most interesting home. Her father, a national celebrity, made his living as a pop singer. His concerts were popular. He cut albums. And he was in high demand for the center of celebrations and social life of the country: weddings.

Being a top wedding singer is a big deal in Arab culture, because Arab weddings are more than two people getting married. (We sometimes wondered where the folk who were getting married were.) It's more like two families getting married spread over weeks. It's Christmas, Fourth of July and Thanksgiving rolled into one.

This was our dream! What an opportunity. Sarah would get to see things few Americans ever could; Sarah would have opportunities few missionaries dared hope for. What a place of influence.

Wedding season starts in June or July and goes for months. Most are lavish affairs, and every night late into the evening, there's dancing, singing, storytelling and feasting (no drinking, of course, it's a Muslim wedding). Every evening all summer long people reveled at weddings; everyone, that is, but Sarah.

Sohalia asked if she could speak with me at our weekly gatherings at the university. I could tell she felt troubled and nervous. But as is the custom, we talked about various chitchat before she came to the point.

"And now, about Sarah," she said. "We have a problem."

"Oh?" I said.

"Sarah does not want to be with my family."

"What? Why not?"

Sohalia blinked back tears. "She is not going with us to the weddings at night."

"What is she doing?"

"She says she needs her sleep, refuses to attend the weddings, and she goes to bed."

As Sohalia fought back the tears, the rest of the story came tumbling out. The parties didn't suit Sarah. They went too late, and she said she needed her sleep. She didn't want to take the afternoon siesta like everyone else. To make matters worse, Sohalia saw the other students' growing friendships. "They are having fun," she said. "All she does is listen to her music."

"She . . ." Sohalia looked out the window, "she doesn't like our country, and she doesn't like me."

When I spoke with Sarah, I got the same story but with a completely different read.

The schedule was awful. She needed her sleep and down time, and she didn't like sleeping during the day as the family did. It was too hot, and Sohalia wanted to walk everywhere. She felt smothered by her hosts, who wanted to be with her all the time. She hated the parties and saw them as a waste of time—besides, nobody spoke English. For that matter, she didn't like their music and thought it sounded demonic.

I talked with Sarah about culture shock and how we cope, but it became clear she felt bad emotions came from a bad culture, not from something simply being different. She felt certain that if you are spiritually strong, you skip culture shock. She was under attack, she said, but God was sustaining her though her Christian music.

Is it any wonder that when Sarah told her family she was a Christian, they were less than impressed? Sarah lost her voice to Sohalia and her family.

Sarah confirms our sense that those most at risk in other cultures are those who are self-righteous. Toward the end of the program, she didn't even want to relate to us. She mostly wore her Walkman and listened to Christian music. The stunning thing to me was the person who seemed to least know that she had missed a wonderful opportunity was Sarah. In her final report she talked about how she knew the missionary life was hard but how this trip had confirmed her call as a missionary. She returned home as a hero in her church for doing missions in the 10/40 window.

Her story is heartbreaking because of the incredible opportunities missed: in witnessing to Muslims and in Sarah's heart too. Even now as I write this, I find myself wishing this wasn't true, but not only is it true, it's repeated time and again. People hit culture shock and decide, based on their negative emotions, that the culture is bad. Then they isolate, criticize and condemn. Often these are the people who are most seen as experts back home since, in our culture, the fastest way to become an expert is to criticize.

We said strong feelings in reaction to cultural differences are inevitable. Frustration, misunderstanding, confusion, tension, embarrassment, repulsion—those things Leeann felt in the Masai hut are the same things Sarah felt in an Arab home. Everyone feels these things. It's the natural process of entering a culture. The important thing now is to look at how we respond to the negative feelings.

Redlining or greenlining describes the two responses to our feelings of culture shock. Redlining is our negative external response to our negative internal feelings. I feel embarrassed, so I pout. I feel frustrated and angry, so I criticize. I feel misunderstood and defensive, so I blame others. I feel confused, so I withdraw.

Redlining is the response Peter's short term received from the church in Jerusalem:

> The apostles and the brothers throughout Judea heard that the Gentiles also had received the word of God. So when Peter went up to Jerusalem, the circumcised believers criticized him and said, "You went into the house of uncircumcised men and ate with them." (Acts 11:1-3)

This is natural. The most common reaction to a negative emotion is a negative action. But because our perceptions in other cultures are so often mistaken, we can easily respond negatively to something that is in truth an open door. If unchecked, this has a spiraling negative effect in two areas. First, it alienates us from our hosts by tearing down trust; second, it causes us to withdraw from the culture and isolate ourselves.

If allowed to continue, we end up as an outsider. We have withdrawn ourselves, or we have offended and been shut out—or both. Redlining is detrimental to the proclamation and acceptance of the gospel. It causes us to lose our voice, just like Sarah.

Be on your guard for redlining. The move from culture shock to redlining is very fluid. It happens in seconds. It's something to check in ourselves daily. You can make many mistakes in culture, but please, don't make this one. It's a nonthinking response, or even worse, a self-righteous one. It is destructive to you and for a gospel witness.

Greenlining is experiencing culture shock and using it as an opportunity to continue to build trust or to learn more about the culture. To greenline is to have a better understanding of how to share the gospel in a different context. To greenline is to take the feelings of discord and use it as a learning moment.

Think back to Leeann's experience in the Masai hut. If repulsed by the smoke in their house, how could she have dealt with these feelings in a way that would have built trust with these Masai women? Maybe she could have asked questions that would have helped her appreciate their choice. She could have asked (and she did ask over time), "Why is the fire inside the house?" Maybe she could have observed some of the advantages of smoke in the home: no flies for one, no malaria for another. Or maybe she could have watched and listened to the ways they interacted with their children and gained a more complete picture of how they love children in their culture. If we are going to speak the gospel to the people of another culture, it is critical that we push through difficult emotional reactions to cultural differences and cope with our feelings in a way that continues to build relationship rather than destroy it.

This takes a certain amount of creativity. Redlining is the easy way out; greenlining requires working to understand rather than to discount. It requires us to learn to appreciate rather than to criticize. It requires us to move toward the culture rather than insulate ourselves from it. It requires us to again take on the humility of Christ.

So we adopt the attitude of Christ as a servant and learner, both as we enter into a culture and again after we have been confronted with it. We continue to ask how can we build bridges for the gospel. Peter provides a helpful model. Reread Acts 10 and notice the practical steps he took when confronted with cultural differences.

Peter was willing to see people though God's eyes and not his own. Pray that God would remind you of the heart he's given you for these people and of his concern for their salvation. Pray to see them through his eyes and not from your Western eyes.

Peter asked the prior question of trust. He was able to articulate how God had changed his heart. Be able to name your emotions. Those who redline quickest are those who are unable to name emotions. They think they have named emotions when they say, "I feel tired."

God reassured Peter that it was okay to be unassuming. Don't assume that someone was intending to hurt you or embarrass you or frustrate you or repulse you. Extend a gracious and generous benefit of doubt.

It required some bravery on Peter's part to travel with his hosts, then meet with them in their home. Be intentional in going forward rather than backwards. Take a deep breath and a moment to think through your reaction. Meet them on their turf. Be brave.

Peter opened his eyes and observed. What do you notice? How are people acting? Talk with them. What do they do in certain situations? What patterns do you observe? Begin to imitate some of the things you observe. Fine-tune your observations. Start over.

Peter asked questions. We say it again: ask lots of questions. Make sure your questions are open-ended and not condescending. Listen carefully to the answers and ask for more clarification. Seek many people's opinions, not just one host or one missionary.

Peter went with a team, but he did not use the team to isolate himself. Don't retreat to the comfort of your team. Setting up a little America is a constant temptation. Sure it's fun to hunt for McDonald's in downtown Kunming, but is that really why you went on a missions trip?

These seven things help us cope when we encounter culture shock.

*   *   *

Leeann and the children had just left for the open-air market when a knock on the door interrupted my writing. Julie stood, bedraggled, on our doorstep. She was with us in the Middle East on the same team as Sarah. Her bright red hair shone against the blazing whitewashed wall of our building.

"Julie! What are you doing here?" I asked, surprised that she had made the trip across town.

"Mack, I'm so exhausted. I need rest. Could I come in and grab some time in a room by myself?"

During our summer we had a small flat in an industrial neighborhood of a metropolitan city. Our neighbors thought us strange and watched our every move. In Arab culture it would not do for me to be alone with a woman in our house.

"Julie, I'm sorry. Leeann's not here, so I can't let you in. They already think we're immoral."

Julie immediately broke down and began to weep. Right there on the street. Not a little tear or two, but head back, mouth open, flood of tears bawling.

Men entering the mosque across the street for afternoon prayers glanced our way.

"Well, okay. You can come in," I capitulated, momentarily losing all concern for cultural sensitivity.

Julie said, through her sobs, "No, no, I understand. I really do. I just didn't expect that."

"Julie, what's going on?" I asked.

"Nothing really bad," she sniffed, "I just can't take never having any space. Mohammed and Chevez won't let me be by myself. They're really sweet, but they think it's evil to be alone. You wouldn't believe what I had to go through just to get across town."

This, we discovered, was one of the hardest things for all Americans in this culture, not just for Sarah. Though Julie was extroverted, she was coming to understand just how individualistic American culture truly is.

"I'm sorry, Julie. You need to remember it's not bad; it's just a different culture. It's really how they're showing that they care for you."

"Yeah," she said. "I know." Then she began weeping again.

Easy for me to say, I thought to myself. I didn't have a host with me literally every waking minute.

"Julie, you know if we were in the States, I would give you a big hug right now, and you're just going to have to imagine it." I said.

Julie took a big breath and gathered herself, "OK, I'll try."

Julie didn't mean she was going to try to imagine a hug; she meant she was going to try to remember that it was a different culture.

I remember watching Julie trudge back toward the train station, wondering if she was going to survive, much less build a bridge of trust.

But she did it, plus much more. What a difference trying makes. Julie experienced the same struggle as Sarah, but she asked questions; she observed; she experimented. Things didn't get easy all at once. But over time she built trust. She took the opportunity to build friendships despite the struggles. Julie greenlined. Was it hard? Absolutely. Julie shed many more tears than the ones that day on my doorstep. Was it worth it? Without a doubt. When she shared her faith with both Mohammed and Chevez, though they did not become Christians, they were intrigued and challenged by Julie's faith since they respected her. And because of these powerful encounters, when Julie returned home, she prepared herself for missions work to Muslim lands. She got her master's degree in Teaching English as a Second Language. Julie works in the Middle East, and God is using her to bring the gospel in a land so close and yet so far from him. Julie's a real hero. She greenlined through culture shock.

12

Scars

Date sent: Fri, 12 Jun 1998 13:07:57-0700
To: Prayer Team
From: Mack Stiles<Mack.Stiles@world.net.com>
Subject: Nebaj, Guatemala

I'm sending e-mail from the home of a family who owns a phone here in Nebaj. Their phone allows for a business: they charge people who come to their house to use it—judging from the lines I wait in, they're doing pretty well. (The folks in line are fascinated by my laptop.) Nebaj is rustic; I'm actually typing while chickens wander from the courtyard though the waiting room to the dirt road outside. There is only one paved street in Nebaj, the rest are dirt—or I should say mud, since the rains started last week. Leeann and the boys and I are living in a 12 x 12 room. A bit cramped for five, but hey, we're happy. It seems like the Ritz after hiking into villages and sleeping in whatever we could find last week.

We worked with the local believers in the villages and our missionary partner, Mike McComb, on an evangelistic outreach in the surrounding mountains. God is at work. We've seen the growth of these small churches from around two or three families to fifteen to twenty families over the past two years. Our job is to act out a number of parables with an Ixil narrator—a big hit. Our teams perform skits, teach simple Bible stories and give testimonies. But our best role, the truth be known, is to be an oddity to gather the villagers, who then stay to hear the powerful preaching of Pablo and Mike. Talk about being fools for Christ.

The poverty and its accompanying ignorance is heartbreaking—we saw an outbreak of pink eye among the children (and some adults), but we've sent back a team to get the medicines to them. The cost is nominal for the treatment, but they didn't know to ask for help. I was grateful to God that we were there.

The tragedy of the war here is far more heartbreaking than pink eye. Close to one third of the Ixil people, about thirty thousand, were murdered here, so there is no one who didn't experience travesties and/or commit them. We met a Christian woman who was full of the Lord, and when I commented on the vibrancy of her faith, Kris, a missionary I was with, pointed out the bullet scars in her arms. An army patrol shot her sons though her arms as she tried to protect them. They were just boys, but the army had shoot-to-kill orders. To picture her sons murdered before her very eyes, and to think of the bullets shattering her arms as she pleaded for their lives, I find beyond imagination.

*　　*　　*

Poverty, ignorance, disease, war crimes, ethnic hatred and racism, murder and genocide—all in the first half of my first letter (the other half is at the end of the chapter).

Short-term missions often serve as a wakeup call to the injustices in the world around us: the hazy awareness from the evening news transformed into grizzly reality.

Sometimes we face a tendency to be defeated on short terms with this overwhelming avalanche of wrong. Any one of the injustices I alluded to in my letter can so stagger our senses we ignore what we see—it's the temptation akin to dozing back to sleep after the wakeup call comes. But faced with all the injustices together, our wakeup call can knock us into the unconscious moral state of hopelessness and despair.

And it's easy to begin thinking it's hopeless when confronted with the poverty of Calcutta, the wars of Central Africa, the systemic racism of America's inner cities, the centuries of ethnic strife in Eastern Europe . . . the list is endless.

After all, what can one short-term program do?

Not much if we don't believe God. But God says he stands against injustice and oppressors (Ps 146:5-10). Nor has he forgotten the victims (Ps 11:5, 7). He says, in his hands, we become instruments against injustice (Ezek 22:25, 27, 30). He says he executes his justice through his might and his Spirit, not our might (Zech 4:6). If we believe God, there is much a short term can do.

Perhaps it comes as a surprise for some to think that avoidance and denial could even happen on a short-term mission. After all, isn't that what we do: proclaiming good news while doing good deeds (Mt 5:14-16)? Yes, but sometimes it's easy to do that and still gloss over issues of injustice that underlie why we are even there in the first place.

Here are three steps that need to be a part of all short-term preparation. These are things we can to do on short-term missions so that we see injustice and evil for what it is:

1. Cultivate a compassionate heart.

2. Develop an understanding of what the Bible says about injustice.

3. Be willing to take action.

Cultivating a Compassionate Heart

Don't go back to sleep after a wakeup call. Develop your compassion during the short term and when you get home. Compassion keeps us awake.

Ken stared mournfully into the bright afternoon sky. He

spoke more to the heavens above than to me.

"Mack," he said, still looking up and trying to hold back tears, "what should I do? This little girl is breaking my heart."

Our worship with the Redeemed Gospel Church ended minutes before. As we waited for our bus, we watched the parishioners stream through the open flaps of the enormous tent back to their homes in the slums of Nairobi. But Ken saw more. He saw a leper for the first time.

Behind him on the curb sat a girl no more than ten years old. Her skin disease had eaten away most of her hair, and there were infectious wounds oozing puss on her neck and head. One hand shaded her eyes from the sun, and the other was held, palm upwards, hoping for a handout from a churchgoer. She smoothed her ragged blue dress across her pencil thin legs and waited, hopefully.

"I don't want to foster a lifestyle of begging . . . you know . . ." said Ken, repeating his middle-class mantra.

"Ken, look. That's just 'insulation' talk. Jesus is not going to berate you when you get to heaven for having mercy on a poor sick child in the slums of Kenya—no matter what the money goes for. Do what God has put in your heart."

I don't know how much Ken gave to that young girl. I wouldn't be surprised if he emptied his wallet (as I had just done in the Redeemed Gospel Church's offering).

Yes, I know. We should give though recognized vehicles that will make sure the money is distributed in proper ways to the proper people in proper amounts. I'm for it, so usually we try to give wisely through organizations. But acting as if spare change to beggars is going to give rise to some new problem for the poor grossly underestimates the problems of the poor. Give first because God has placed compassion in your heart rather than for some effect. Sometimes in our desires to make sure we're not being ripped off or supporting something bad, we deaden compassion. God wants soft hearts more than efficient remedies; a compassionate heart gives us eyes to see and keeps us awake to the world.

Develop an Understanding of What the Bible Says About Injustice
"Make no mistake: nothing challenges one's faith and hope in God like the rank evil of naked injustice. And nothing short of the authoritative, divine Word of God will withstand its withering scorn."[1] So writes Gary Haugen in his outstanding book *Good News About Injustice,* which we think should be required reading for all short terms.

What's the good news about injustice? God hates it, says Haugen. To know the Scriptures is to know that God is compassionate (Ps 145:9) and a just judge (1 Sam 2:9-10) who seeks rescue for victims (Is 59:14-16).

> He will guard the feet of his saints, but the wicked will be silenced in darkness. It is not by strength that one prevails; those who oppose the LORD will be shattered. He will thunder against them from heaven; the LORD will judge the ends of the earth. He will give strength to his king and exalt the horn of his anointed. (1 Sam 2:9-10)

How does God seek rescues? Does he do it for everyone all the time? Why doesn't he step in and do more? I don't know. But I do walk between three rock-solid understandings: I believe in God on a cross, I believe judgment will come beyond judgment on earth, and I believe he wants me to be involved in the solution.

A God on a cross. Nietzsche scorned Christians for believing in "a God on a cross." But I find what he saw as our weakness to be one of the most amazing strengths of our faith. We believe in one who has so closely identified with us that he shared in our misery and tasted our death.

Judgment will come. We fully support justice in the here and now. But it's clear we can't apportion justice perfectly, either. One day God will judge the world, and then the justice we long to see in the world and experience only in bits and pieces will be done in full and done perfectly. There is more than what we see. For now, Jesus tells us, the wheat and tares grow together (Mt 13:24-30).

Take Action

God wants his people involved in the solution. That will prove difficult if we lack compassion and a biblical understanding of injustice, but impossible if we are unwilling to take action. Keep eyes and ears open; don't ignore the issues on short-term programs. If you're on a missions trip to the inner city, don't just paint a house, deal with issues of racism. In the slums of the Philippines, look at the forces that made them that way. We're not calling for a resolution of these problems, but a recognition that they exist. These are complex, difficult issues. Good people disagree on solutions, but ignorance and denial is unacceptable.

Next, teach about injustice from the Bible, if you are in a position to do so. For example, I'm amazed at how often the Bible teaches on dealing with the issues of racism and how seldom we hear about it. Peter's journey to Cornelius's house involved dealing with the issues of racism, and Luke goes to pains to record the story twice. But seldom do we hear about the steps God took to rid Peter of his racist attitudes.[2] The heart of Peter's story with Cornelius is God's dealing with Peter's racism; yet for years I was as blind to that as Peter was to his own racism.

Finally, everyone needs to tell stories of the victims of oppression they encounter.

There were twenty people gathered in our house for a party when Julia called.

"Mack, are you busy?"

Julia had attended one of the first short terms we led to the highlands of Guatemala, the site of the Guatemalan civil war. She had become a friend of our family. But this was no friendly call; she sounded agitated.

"Well, we've got some friends over . . ."

But Julia was in no mood for hints.

"That's okay. I won't take long," she said. "You know, I've been taking Latin-American studies since I got back from Guatemala, and I'm pretty upset about our short-term program."

"What? How so?"

"I've been reading about the Guatemala civil war, and I just feel like we need to prepare the students better."

"Okay . . . what do you mean?" I felt defensive.

"Well, we just didn't know what happened there."

I paused for breath. "Julia, you were the one who most wanted to stop the training and get on with 'real' missions work."

"Yeah, I know."

"And Julia, you know I want our folk to be prepared," I said.

She sighed and said in a softer tone, "Yeah, I know. It's that the war there was just so horrible, and I didn't have a clue when I was there."

I felt softer too as I remembered passing concrete slab after concrete slab, each representing a family burned off their land; the mass graves, each representing a village genocide; faces and names of orphans, each representing murdered parents. I knew I had no reason to be defensive. Julia was on to something.

"Julia, you're doing what I hope all of our short-term people do: you've been serious about your experience by taking classes, working on a language and really thinking about going back."

"That's true," she said.

"So thanks, and I want to tell you that I'll try to do better."

Haugen says the way injustice continues is for good people to say nothing. There is no room for moral ambiguity when we face real injustice. Injustice is aggressive and ready to defend itself. We should be just as ready to stand against injustice and speak out.

Use your professional skills. Just as the most powerful evangelism may come from the one who pulled the tooth, so the one to give the greatest credibility to a story may be the dentist who speaks out back home.

Think about developing skills to help. After Kim saw the malnourishment clinic we worked at in Guatemala, she returned home and changed her major to dietetics, planning on returning as a full-time missionary.

And finally, when you encounter a serious issue of injustice, contact International Justice Mission on the Web at <www.ijm.org> for further help and information.

What can one small short term do? Quite a bit. That's because of who our God is and what he does. Remember the Lord.

The rest of the letter from Nebaj:

But when I see that woman's joy in Christ here in the Ixil area, I'm reminded that the ability of the gospel to heal is beyond our imagination too. Jesus has scars much like the scars on that woman's arms. In fact, the longer I'm here, the thing I find most amazing about this beautiful place is not the horrific violence but the power of the gospel to bring healing, hope and love.

Just three evenings ago we had church in the village (classic Ixil church: tin roof, boards on cinder blocks for pews, bad PA system hooked to a car battery). I sat between Pablo and Calixstro in a worship service. Pablo scouted for the army (after being hunted by them himself), and Calixstro fought with the guerillas.

Calixstro murdered forty men during the war who were suspected of being informants. He killed them with his bare hands since the guerillas saved their bullets for the army. Years later Calixstro found the faces of the men he killed haunting his dreams in their various stages of death. When he met our missionary friend, Mike, he wanted to know, "Can your God forgive me?"

When Calixstro came to Christ two years ago, do you know who discipled him? Yep, it was Pablo, his former enemy.

I can't describe what it was like to worship God between these two men. Can Jesus forgive us? ... Oh yes, he can. As they say here, "Gloria a Dios!" Praise God. Where else is there such a great salvation? Where will the world turn for reconciliation but to Jesus?

The students are a great team this year: hard working, compassionate, full of Jesus. They're also a bit sick. About half the team caught a Guatemalan bug that put them in bed (and in the outhouse) for a couple of days. Nothing serious, but pray we'll get better.

I hope this e-mail gets out. If not, I'll tell you all about it when I get home.

In Christ's care,

Mack and Leeann

13

Headlines from Mombasa

*WHEN OUR PROGRAM RECEIVED OFFICIAL APPROVAL FROM THE MINIS-*try of education in a Muslim country, we agreed not to evangelize openly. But we also agreed that topics of respective faiths were not out-of-bounds. We focused on the fact that we would come with a program that would develop their students' English skills but made sure to tell them we desired for our students to have conversations about culture and faith. It was a rare chance to share Christian faith in a Muslim context.

A Call for Boldness

Michelle, a student from Duke University, spent her summer with Nada, an English major from a Middle Eastern university. Nada's English improved dramatically. Her curiosity about Christianity grew too.

During the last days of the program Nada opened her heart to Michelle, telling her of her fears of death, the doubts she had about the Muslim faith and the despair she felt of ever knowing God.

Michelle and I talked of this conversation on the plane ride home.

"And Mack," she said, "sometimes she so despaired of ever knowing God that she thought about ending her life."

"Michelle, that's incredible!" I said, "What an opportunity. So what did you say about Jesus?"

Michelle looked down at her hands folded on top of her seatbelt buckle. "Well, I . . . I guess I was just too scared."

I felt my stomach drop, though the plane remained perfectly level. It was an opportunity some spend their entire lives in Muslim countries to know—an opportunity missed.

I don't see it as Michelle's fault. It is too easy for us to focus on getting visas and airplane tickets, garnering enough support and the right shots, or even working on cultural sensitivity, while forgetting to prepare to share our faith. To go on a short-term mission without being prepared to share our faith is like inviting people to a banquet while forgetting to serve the food.

Since that trip, Leeann and I have made some changes in our prefield orientation. We have tried to better prepare our participants to share their faith in a crosscultural setting. We believe this requires a commitment to bold contextual evangelism:[1] *bold* because many seem ready to sling a hammer yet petrified of sharing their faith and *contextual* because those who have a desire for evangelism often utilize methods popular at home but which don't communicate in a different culture.

A Call for Contextualization

The *Daily Nation*, the national newspaper of Kenya, breathlessly reported that a major American Christian denomination would be sending hundreds to Mombasa on Kenya's east coast. They were coming for two weeks. The report detailed travel itinerary, which included time for trips to game parks and shopping in the local markets. They would be staying in beach hotels, and "the local populous would be expected to give the Americans a hearty Kenyan welcome."

The *Nation* reported that the Americans would be distributing literature and "Kenyans of all faiths were encouraged to be supportive of their efforts." Then the paper gave a breakdown of the amount of money the "tourists" would be generating for the local economy by category: airfare—14,000 Kenyan shillings; hotel—5,000 Kenyan shillings; and so on. After a slap on the back for a certain member in the tourist affairs office who landed the "contract," the article reported a running total of how much money the tourist agency generated year-to-date.

When the Americans arrived (you guessed it), stories circulated among the group of the amazing success they experienced with the Muslim population in Mombasa. They left with excitement over how easy it was to see Muslims come to Jesus. They felt their trip was fruitful. The response they received seemed the same as for someone who received Christ back home. But was it sincere? When this outreach was followed up, not a single missionary, including those who belonged to that denomination, found one Muslim who actually came to faith.

Sharing faith across cultures is complex. We must take into account the context of others' situations. East African nations need tourism dollars, and this group gave a huge boost to the local economy. But this group was unsuccessful because they gave no thought about how to relate the gospel in a different culture.

Being Bold and Contextual at the Same Time

For evangelism to happen crossculturally, we must be both bold and contextual. Think back to Peter and Cornelius. Peter opened the missionary door to the Gentiles by practicing cultural sensitivity. Peter saw powerful results when he shared the message of the gospel too. Peter astutely builds upon the experience Cornelius has had with God and his head knowledge of the life of Jesus. He then testifies to Jesus as being appointed by God and the source of forgiveness for sin (Acts 10:34-43).

It's clear that Peter understood the point of cultural sensitivity is not to appear culturally sophisticated or simply to avoid offense; it is to communicate the gospel. Like him, we need to be prepared to testify to our faith thoughtfully in light of cultural differences and yet with bold confidence. Here are some ways to get started.

Be bold where you are. The greatest tool in sharing your faith across a culture is to know your own faith. Know the major tenets of what Christians believe. Be able to explain your story of faith. Know how to help people cross the line into faith.

Don't make the common mistake that somehow it will be easier to share your faith there than it is here. Make efforts to share your faith at home. Start praying and looking for opportunities to share your faith. If you begin to develop an evangelistic lifestyle here, it will seem much less foreign in a foreign land.

Pray boldly. Pray for boldness. Just like Paul:

Pray also for me, that whenever I open my mouth, words may be given me so that I will fearlessly make known the mystery of the gospel, for which I am an ambassador in chains. Pray that I may declare it fearlessly, as I should. (Eph 6:19-20)

Anna Gulick is a seventy-five-year-old retired missionary from Japan and one of my prayer supporters.

"Mack," I heard Anna's voice on the other end of the line.

"Yes, Anna," I said. She inhaled, and I braced for my exhortation.

"Mack, I got your prayer letter yesterday, and I wanted you to know that it's all well and good to be praying for the group's safety, but you don't have a single prayer request for the spiritual battle. You don't expect to move out to share your faith and not be opposed, do you?"

"No, Anna," I said, chastened.

"Right, then, you need to get out another letter, and I want you to . . ."

Anna had a number of things more to say, and I'll not recount them, except to say that she's right. Don't leave out prayers for boldness and the spiritual battle.

Tell people that you don't want to offend. Being bold is not a license to offend those to whom we go. Be bold in telling people you don't want to offend.

We stood before a Buddhist temple of an Asian country, a country considered unreached. Festivalgoers packed the temple and grounds that night for a celebration. The gongs gonged, the incense burned, and crowds circled the temple with candles. Lanterns dispelled some of the darkness. Saffron-robed monks huddled in the dark corners in the outside courtyard. Someone handed me a stick of incense, and others swept me into the circling crowd. As we walked, a woman next to me asked in perfect English, "Would you like some help?" Stunned, I said, "You speak English?"

She said, laughing, "Yes, I'm from here, but I attend the University of Virginia."

After we exchanged some pleasantries and met her family, I said, "We do need your help. I'm struggling to understand something. I'm a Christian . . ."

"Yes," she said in a way that meant yes, all Americans are Christians.

"And I don't want to do something here that would offend either Buddhists or my own beliefs in Jesus."

And we were off and running on a wonderful conversation about faith.

Let people know you don't want to offend and you'll find tremendous open doors in unexpected places.

Be in partnership with those who are committed to sharing the gospel. We'll mention this again, but it bears repeating. Ask how the people you partner with in the host country are sharing their faith. Learn from them. Ask them what they would want people to know about evangelism in the place where they live. Make sure plans for evangelism are in concert with your missionary and hosts. And know that sometimes the best evangelism is to support local evangelists.

Do your homework on issues of faith in the local setting. Understand the basic tenets of the host's faith. What parallels do they share with Christianity? Buddhist morality closely parallels Christianity, but Buddhists and Christians are sharply divided when it comes to knowing God. Be able to make these distinctions.

It's also important to know how Westerners in general and Christians more specifically give offense to your host's religious practices.

Third, know the major objections they may have about Christianity. Muslims, for example, are deeply offended by the idea that Jesus was the Son of God, thinking Christians believe God had sex with a human.

Learn the difference between gospel and culture. Too many Americans are unable to make distinctions between what is American and what is gospel. From worship, to the type of clothes someone wears, to the number of wives in a household, we tend to spread our cultural expectations with a veneer of biblical proof texting. The best way to come to grips with this is to leave our culture. But an equally important dynamic is to have a firm grasp of what the Bible says and does not say.

For example, some Americans act as if to be late in an event-oriented culture is a travesty on the order of adultery. What does being on time have to do with Scripture? Sure, you can make a case for it, but there is an equally strong case against time-related anxiety.

Remember that in many ways the Bible speaks more clearly and profoundly to nontechnical societies than it does to the West. We have much to learn from the way other cultures see the truth of the Scripture. We can see, with their help, the materialism, racism, individualism and secularism we are unable to see on our own.

The reason Peter needed a vision from God about his attitudes toward the Gentiles was he could not see it himself. That's one of the miracles of a short term: we gain the vision to distinguish gospel and culture.

Expect the unexpected. As Winfried Corduan notes in his excellent book *Neighboring Faiths,* "Too many evangelicals try to understand other religions on the basis of quick formulas. This is a mistake. Avoid imposing simple schemes on the basis of what the person is *supposed to* believe. For example, many Hindus are not pantheists, many Buddhists do not want to escape into nirvana, and many Jews are not looking for a messiah. Sadly, many Christians do not believe that they are saved by grace though faith."[2] Take time to learn about your host's religious experience as an individual. You may even be surprised, as Peter was with Cornelius, to find God has already begun to reveal himself.

Be bold when you sense the Spirit opening doors. Opportunities to share the gospel come in all sizes. Some may be huge, as when Cornelius and his household asked to hear "everything the Lord has commanded you to tell us" (Acts 10:33). Other times you may have an opportunity to step in and clarify just one point of the gospel. Or you may have the chance to talk about how faith in Jesus has made a difference in your life. Take advantage of each of these openings and wait to see how the Lord will use them.

Be Ready: Sometimes You Will See Great Harvests

During the same year the *Daily Nation* reported of the outreach in Mombasa, we held an outreach too. We paired African evangelists with our short-term participants to share their faith with the village of Kisomas. On the third day of our outreach, God chose to move with power. While his neighbors hung on his fence and looked on, I remember kneeling to pray a prayer of commitment with a man in his garden. At first I thought the onlookers were curious, but then I discovered they wanted to pray to follow Christ too. We didn't have enough people to pray with those who wanted to give their lives to Jesus. By week's end the Anglican church we partnered with began baptizing hundreds of new believers.

Years later people still remember the way God moved at Kisomas. And over the course of our program, years later we would meet Kenyans who came to Christ in the Kisomas outreach. The difference between Kisomas and Mombasa? A response in one culture can mean a very different thing than a response in another, even from one side of the country to another. Another difference may have been our partnerships. We had lived in Kenyan homes before the outreach and knew the food and some of the local customs, at least enough to avoid offense.

Most of the outreach's appeal came from Kenyans noticing our friendships with Kenyan Christians. And God chose to move with power.

The Holy Spirit is like the wind; we don't know where he comes from or where he's going, but sometimes you'll be swept up in his power.

14

Partnerships
Back Home & On-Site

THE CHURCH IN ANTIOCH, WHERE BELIEVERS WERE FIRST CALLED "Christians," was a missions church. They knew what it meant to cross cultures. Before they ever tried to cross the major cultural divide in their world—Greeks and Jews—they had already learned how by being a multiethnic church.

They provided generously for those in need: first with the church in Judea (Acts 11:29-30), then later when they sent Paul and Barnabas as short-term missionaries. In fact, when they sent out Paul and Barnabas, they not only shared their financial resources but their leadership as well. One can only imagine what it was like to lose the teaching and pastoral work of both Paul and Barnabas to an eighteen-month missions trip.

They knew how to celebrate too. When Paul returned from

the missions trip, "they gathered the church together and reported all that God had done through them and how he had opened the door of faith to the Gentiles" (Acts 14:27). What a delightful debrief.

Part of the need for modern missions is churches modeling the things they ask short-term missionaries to do: congregations who make disciples at home and not just among the nations, multiethnic communities who understand the complexities of crossing cultures, churches who are about the work of evangelism and evangelism training. We need fellowships that are generous too, willing to share their financial resources and even their best leaders when the call comes.

Partnership with a Sending Church

The church in Antioch prepared Paul to be sent, supported him when he was gone and helped him return. And it becomes a model for churches today: to commission short termers, support them and then welcome them home. We need churches who will love their short-term missionaries.

But this partnership is a two-way street. We also need short-term missionaries who have a love for the church. Just as Paul loved the church in Antioch, we need missionaries who are connected with a local body, those who see their home fellowships worth reproducing in the places where they are sent.

Too many pastor references cross our desk filled with "can't comment." We have heard too many frustrated pastors who only see short termers when they show up for money. The church is not an adjunct to personal faith but part and parcel of it. No one should expect to help the church grow in other places without a love and understanding of the church where they live.

A sending church needs to be intentional. A commissioning

service, prayer while they're away and some kind of welcome home are a good start. Students International (SI) recommends churches start a short-term mentoring program. Short termers are assigned to a mentor, preferably a mentor who has attended a short term. The mentors serve as prayer partners, coaches and ears upon the short termers' return.

Most importantly, churches that sponsor short terms should include training for every team that goes, including not just what to pack or an overview of the schedule but training on the biblical basis of missions and how to cross a culture with sensitivity.

As a short termer, you need to be responsive to your sending church as well. You should be a committed member and involved in the local missions of the church. You should seek guidance from the leadership of the church about your decision to go on a short-term mission and keep them informed as your plan progresses. Send updates and prayer requests as often as possible while on the missions trip. And on your return, be prepared to give a full report to your church so that they are encouraged by all God has done.

Partnerships with National Christians

When Chuck Ellis founded Students International (SI), a short-term missions organization, he thought matching the interests and gifts of the participants with ministry sites on the field would be cutting edge. But the real impact of SI has not been with ministry sites but rather the way SI formed partnership with Guatemalans.

Students International set up their ministry sites to have both missionaries and Guatemalan Christians who host the students. The students join an ongoing-ministry site. The missionary and national see their job as both ministering to the ongoing project *and* to the short termers. This is where the real impact of the program occurred. Not from the ministry site, as Chuck expected, but from the ministry of the hosts.

Chuck told us, "The struggle on any short-term mission is against the glorified vacation—a sightseeing mentality that produces a relationless trip. So the best part of our program was having students ministered to by their Guatemalan hosts. For Americans to bond with nationals has been the single-best ministry tool of our program. We see this now as the most important part of what we offer short-term missions: a model of missions that can be found in few places—true partnership, from true indigenous leadership."

Chuck serves as a model for us on short-term programs. As we've mentioned previously, such partnerships give us an insider's view and enable us to move quickly from being a bumbling foreigner to an effective ministry either alongside or in a support role of our hosts.[1] They also allow our relationships to continue even when we are not physically present.

Paul modeled partnerships with the people he visited. He lived an interesting life, but he rarely wrote about his travels: the weather during his voyages or how many wild animals he saw as he traveled overland, or the sights of the ancient cities he visited (though he makes reference to all of those things). What Paul *did* write about was relationships: with people and with God.

Read these words Paul wrote to the church he helped start in Thessalonica:

> We loved you so much that we were delighted to share with you not only the gospel of God but our lives as well, because you had become so dear to us. (1 Thess 2:8)

> But Timothy has just now come to us from you and has brought good news about your faith and love. He has told us that you

always have pleasant memories of us and that you long to see us, just as we also long to see you. (1 Thess 3:6)

Remember that Paul's longings and love for the Thessalonians formed after only weeks with this new church. He fills his letters with his love and affection for people he had spent time with on his missions trip, time measured in months or even weeks.

Powerful partnerships still happen today; churches form, life-long friendships do too. And it can happen all in the short weeks of a short-term program. We long for those who go with us on short-term missions to write letters to the people they were with, like Paul's letters.

The practical side of Paul's partnerships includes leadership. Paul quickly appointed indigenous church leaders and had high expectations for them. This often happened as a function of necessity (since Paul had a habit of getting run out of town). But at other times it happened intentionally, as when Paul included Timothy and Titus, both Greeks, in his ministry. Paul never expected to run the churches he established. This has long been a goal of long-term missions, but the best short terms need an indigenous commitment too.

All short-term programs should attempt to form strong partnerships with their sending churches and with the national church. Another key partnership is with missionaries, the subject of our next chapter.

15

Pith Helmets & Modern Missionaries

WHEN MIKE AND TERRI MCCOMB MOVED TO THE CITY OF NEBAJ, Guatemala, and began their work with the Ixil people,[1] they started by using their skills in agriculture. Mike and Terri did this work with a commitment to cultural sensitivity. They rented a house in a neighborhood with locals. Terri wore indigenous dress. Mike purchased some land and began planting crops using modern techniques. Mike didn't preach; he just harvested good crops. Ixil farmers who passed by noticed his good-looking stand of corn and asked him how he got such good yields. Over the years Mike took these opportunities to teach techniques to prevent topsoil runoff or practice crop rotation. Mike began to notice his methods being reproduced in the hills around him. Later Mike started a fish farm using a local popular fish to sell in the market. By introducing more protein into the diets, Mike felt he could prevent some of the endemic malnourishment of the region. He then used proceeds from the fish farm to help a local Christian orphanage and Christian school.

These wonderful and noble achievements would have made for a great missionary career, but as Mike became more conversant in the local culture and language, he longed to do more. So Mike developed a friendship with a local evangelist, Pablo, and began hiking to small surrounding villages to plant churches. This was agriculture of a different kind, but Mike proved as adept at sowing the gospel as he did at crops. The churches took root and began to grow.

Mike says church planting produced tremendous long-term good for the villages surrounding Nebaj. "Deep-rooted, destructive patterns have changed," says Mike. "People who used to beat their wives have become loving husbands, those who practiced violence in civil war have come to love their enemies, and hard hearts have changed forever because of the gospel."

We send short-term teams to work with Mike, Terri and Pablo. We've planted crops on the ag farm, we've built latrines and a sidewalk at the Christian school, and we've helped other local missionaries. We've also taken hikes with Mike and Pablo to the villages for evangelism.

We love Mike's model of missions: he demonstrates a blend of social action, evangelism and indigenous partnership that is a challenge for us. Planting crops and planting churches both serve to answer the prayer "Thy kingdom come; thy will be done on earth as it is in heaven."

Missionaries are some of the most wonderful people we know. And if you want to have a good short-term experience, you need to learn to love them too. Often they are the ones who make it possible for you to be there in the first place. And they are one of the keys to a good trip. But some short-term programs avoid missionaries altogether, seeming to forget that the only way to return to a country is as a missionary.

Do missionaries seem hopelessly out of date on the latest evangelistic methods? Yes, they've been worried about how to get a church planted in a village that has a 100 percent illiteracy rate.

Are they behind the times on the latest worship songs? Sure, they've been figuring out tonal structures for songs that don't even sound like songs to us.

Do they seem unconcerned with the bout of diarrhea in the group? Well, after struggling with bilharzia and dengue fever in the last year, it just doesn't seem like that big of a deal.

Really, the biggest problem with missionaries is us. Elisabeth Elliot comments that our use of language tends to glorify missionaries. When people write about missionaries, she notes, they use mythical language. "Missionaries don't 'go,' they 'go forth'; missionaries don't 'walk,' they 'tread the burning sands'; missionaries don't 'die,' they 'lay down their lives.'"[2] With this cultural hype it's no wonder we don't know how to treat missionaries when we meet a real live one. Many unfairly place missionaries on pedestals. When it's discovered that missionaries are ordinary people with ordinary problems, respect for missionaries comes crashing down. Yes, most missionaries I know are heroes but only because they are ordinary people with an extraordinary God. Here are some tips about forming partnerships with missionaries.

Be helpful. Be considerate and helpful. Expect to work hard without complaining. Ask them before you arrive about what you can bring to help them. Take them items they can't get. (We limit our participants to one piece of baggage so that we can use the carry on and other bag to take stuff for the mission. This has produced some interesting conversations with customs officials, especially when we took airplane props and electronic equipment.) Take packages home for them. Have your church support them financially and with prayer.

Learn all you can from them. Interview missionaries about missions. Ask them how their expectations were different from the realities. Ask the best way to prepare. Don't update them on the latest missiological trends or correct them on the proper ways of contextualized evangelism, but find out the history of the missions work in the area and their plans for the future.

Missionaries have stepped out of our culture and can often see us more through eyes of the national, so ask, "What can we do to change?" They see things we can't.

Participate in ongoing projects. Come alongside the work missionaries are doing rather than making a special project just for your short term. Mike McComb was getting ready to shut down his work with short terms until he got the good idea of letting the short-term participants go with him on his hikes to help build the church plants in the Ixil area. What he allowed us to do was become involved in his program, not create more work by setting up a special ministry for us.

Mike also farmed us out to a local church to work on their building and to other missionaries to work on their projects. See if you can have partnerships with a number of different missionaries, as we did in Nebaj, to spread the work around.

Watch your expectations of what a missionary should do. Few people think of missionaries as people with pith helmets and machetes nowadays, but stereotypes still exist. No matter what a missionary does, understand that the best missionaries aren't good because of their job, they're good because of their attitude toward the culture in which they live.

Waldo doesn't fit the classic understanding of what missionaries do. He fixes airplane radios used for missionary service in Kenya. He works in the hangar all day long. He didn't need to learn a language to do his job, but he learned Swahili. He also became an elder in a local African church rather than attend the church with the expatriate community. He has African friends to his house; he eats ugali, the Kenyan dish. Although Waldo isn't a traditional missionary, he's still a good model.

Good missionaries use public transportation at times (especially if that is the kind of transportation most of the people they work with use). They speak the language; they eat the food. They have friendships and respect for the nationals they work with. Look for these kinds of missionaries as models of cultural sensitivity. Be gracious though; remember that missionaries are on a journey too.

Be respectful of their long-term investments in a locale. Missionaries have a lot at stake with you being there. You get to leave; they can't. Sometimes their reputation or even their ability to stay is at stake. It is important that we as short termers be extremely respectful of this.

The heat was the first thing I noticed when I stepped off the plane. A brittle heat radiated from the baked tarmac and from bleached buildings, a heat so powerful that each gust of wind felt more akin to the exhaust of a bus than an offer of comfort. Welcome to the Middle East. I felt jet lagged and sad: it was Father's Day and I was missing my kids. I also knew no one in the entire country and felt very alone. You can imagine my joy when I saw a man holding a sign for "Mack." Kevin, a tentmaker missionary, met with me for fifteen minutes outside customs in the airport.

"Here is a list of potential contacts at the university," he said.

"Thanks," I said.

"Here is how you catch the public transportation," he said.

"Okay," I said with disappearing hopes that he might give me a lift.

"Now remember, we haven't met, okay? I know you understand," he said without waiting for my response.

He had written the lists and instructions in careful handwriting, and he took off. I understood. He had a lot at stake. Still, it was hard watching him leave.

It seemed foolish to be there since nobody had done what we wanted to do: establish a short-term program with the full awareness of the officials that we were a Christian group. We would teach English, but it would be well known that we were a Christian organization. Some told us with that approach it would be just as likely as allowing a Muslim fundamentalist to teach at Southern Baptist Seminary. Others said it was plain dangerous. Kevin was willing to help us, but even our short meeting in the airport put him in a precarious position.

But in a matter of days the Lord had worked, and I signed a contract with government officials for the first program of its kind. I'm still astounded at this miraculous event. And I'm glad Kevin took the risks he did—it couldn't have happened without him. I'm also glad that our program didn't endanger the good work he continues to do in that country.

Remember that bad missionaries are the exception. The vast majority of missionaries are self-sacrificing, hard-working, godly people. But there are bad missionaries: some live embarrassingly affluent lifestyles, others harbor patronizing, almost racist, attitudes about the very people they work with, some have built works that can't survive without them or the money they bring in. They are the exceptions. One bad missionary does not make all bad.

Missionaries need to understand short terms just like anyone else. Many have not had the time to think through a thoughtful biblical view of short terms and see them in much the same way as some in the Christian community.

They need to know that short terms are not just a way to increase their workload but a function of call and careful partnerships between hosts, participants and missionary. Give them this book. Outline the training your short term gives the participants. Involve them in your orientation if possible. Have them share their testimonies about how they heard God's call in their lives.

Good short terms stand on three legs: partnerships with a sending church, partnerships with hosts and partnerships with missionaries. All three need to be strong and in good balance for your trip to reach its fullest potential. But even with all these in place, there is a certain amount of risk inherent in all short terms—risks known and unknown. In the next chapter we'll consider the costs of risk.

16

Unnecessary Risk?

DR. BRANHAM CALLED ME WITH A REQUEST. "MR. STILES, AS YOU know, my daughter is going on your program to Africa. I'm *not* excited about this, but I've decided I'll let her go if you will guarantee her safety."

My response was immediate. "I can't do that Dr. Branham."

"I won't be having my daughter going on a trip with people who won't guarantee her safety," he said.

"Dr. Branham, this is a missions trip, not a sightseeing tour. The only promise I can make is that it's dangerous."

"That's unacceptable to me."

"Then, Dr. Branham, I don't think your daughter should go either," I said.

Dr. Branham wasn't ready for that. "Well, I . . . um," he said.

"I'll send her a rejection notice for the program. We have a waiting list, so it will be no problem to refund her money," I said. Then I added, "But Dr. Branham, I think you're discouraging your daughter from becoming the kind of person you want her to be—someone who is willing to risk to help others."

Risk makes our stomachs ball up every year we direct a short-term program. And the more we go the more aware we become of real risks involved, risks that others might not even notice.

*   *   *

I didn't start thinking about my conversation with the ticket agent until KLM flight 902 from the Middle East to Amsterdam leveled at cruising altitude.

"Mr. Stiles," he had said, "we cannot match your bags with your tickets, so I've given you an extra baggage claim. It's no problem. All your bags are on the plane. You'll just need to remember when you get to Amsterdam, you'll have one extra baggage stub."

One extra stub didn't seem too much to carry. I smiled and said it was not a problem. I just wanted to make the plane. After all, they only flew once a week.

But when the flight leveled, his words came back to me with chilling clarity. I sat bolt upright in my seat. If I had an extra stub, it meant someone else could load a bag on our plane that looked like one we checked, but it could contain anything—anything!

I wished I had grabbed that agent by his shirt and demanded every bag be unloaded and rechecked or we would not get on the plane. I sweated every minute of that flight.

When we landed in Amsterdam, I felt foolish for worrying. Security seemed fine, and I just got a little worked up. That is until I opened my paper the following week, safe in my home, and discovered the same flight, flight 902, had been hijacked by a Muslim fundamentalist. Was something fishy going on the week before? Had we narrowly missed something? Who knows? It's a risk we take.

We wish Jesus called us to live in personal peace and security. We wish we could proclaim his message over the Internet or the TV. But that's not how he came; it's not what he did. He lived with people who risked their lives in an unsafe world.

*   *   *

I stopped the car after a line of cars going the other way flashed their lights and honked at me. Nobody seemed to be driving our way. A man waving his arms ran to us while we sat on the side of the road.

"Bwana, please turn around and go home. There are riots here, and people will take your life and the life of your family," he said, pointing to our children in the back of the car. "Hurry!"

I turned the old African car around. It sputtered and almost died. At the same moment four men sprang from some brush on the side of the road with machetes raised. The car chugged again as one man hit the trunk with his blade. Two more grabbed for the door handles. But the car, as if realizing its own danger, roared to life, and we sped to safety. Our children slept the entire time.

We don't always know what it is we're risking. Life itself is risky. Leaving home might even be risky.

*   *   *

Leeann repeatedly asked her father to talk louder. Not only did they have a bad connection, but the afternoon call to prayer from the mosque started as soon as she (finally) got through. In a few moments she gently hung up the receiver and stared at the phone. Tears trickled down her cheeks, and though I asked, "Honey, what's wrong?" I knew. Her fear had come true. Leeann's grandmother had died while we were away. One of the most important persons in Leeann's life was gone, and she would not be there for the funeral to honor her grandmother or be with the rest of her family in their time of grief.

Even if we could manage risk in every possible situation, there still would be somebody who didn't believe or wouldn't listen.

*   *   *

We told Jim not to go to the Park of the Cross in Antigua, Guatemala; we told him not to go out alone; we told him not to take his stuff with him. At least he wasn't out after dark. But broad daylight didn't stop the three guys in black hoods who jumped him with razor knives. He was alone in the park with everything he owned in his backpack. Fortunately, he didn't struggle. "If he had," said a bored policeman, "it would have been . . ." then the policeman ran his index finger across his throat.

*   *   *

Sometimes we risk because of spiritual realities others just can't see. This is the hardest risk to take. We do it because we believe that Jesus is more "real" than the "real world."

We were studying the Bible with a group of Muslims in the heart of an Arab city. Ten of us sat in a circle in an open courtyard. It was morning, but the rising sun already began blistering the white stucco walls. For the Muslims in the group, it was their first Bible study. I read Luke 10 and began asking questions, but Henda, so taken with the text, took over the leadership of the group: "Look!" she said, "This man bound his wounds. He put him on his own beast. He paid for his stay in the inn with his own money!"

As she spoke, I saw a glint of light and raised my head just in time to see a bottle flash from the apartment complex two stories above us and land with a dull thud in a flowerpot on the edge of the courtyard. It landed in the only place it could have landed without hitting someone or shattering into a thousand glass splinters. The city noises masked its fall. Nobody noticed but me. I held my two year old on my lap—my first thought was for his safety, then for the safety of the others. But as the words to flee formed in my mouth, God spoke to my heart, "You are safe where you sit—don't move."

Henda continued, "What kind of man is this?" she asked. "What is this about? What does this mean?" she stared at her new Bible. Clearly the Spirit was at work in this young Muslim woman, and I was not to interrupt with my small concerns for our safety from flying bottles.

* * *

Sometimes we risk because we are ignorant about how things are done. We have no clue we're risking in the first place.

I forced my body, wracked with amebic dysentery, to crawl on all fours to the bathroom. I remember the cool, smooth Kenyan concrete on my face as I paused in weakness on my thirty-foot journey. I had lost twenty-five pounds in one week. What a diet! The plague caused two stages of misery: first, fear that I might die; next, fear that I might not. *I wish I hadn't drunk that water,* I said to myself. But we had traveled all day long on that hot dusty road, and so when Mrs. Mwitte gave me a glass of water, I gulped it down before Kishoyian asked where they got it and then left his glass untouched. All I could do was stare at my empty cup and wait.

* * *

We're not thrill seekers. We don't risk as people who do dangerous adventure travel for a rush. I don't drive down the road without a seatbelt because it's exciting, I do it because many cars around the globe don't have seatbelts (and I haven't found any on the back of flatbed trucks).

The thing that stood out to me about my driver of the "taxi" was his bright, gold front tooth. I spent most of the trip wishing I couldn't see it, since I wanted him to stop turning to smile at me and to watch his driving. We hurtled down a twisty road at 80 to 90 miles an hour. I thought, *Next time I see metal braces and pins on a driver's legs, I'll find another cab.* We passed a car on a blind curve. *The system is the problem,* I thought to myself philosophically. The two other passengers squeezed in the backseat with me chatted amicably in Arabic. *Since they're paid by the head, the more they take and the faster they go, the more they make,* I reasoned. The lines on the highway flashed by like dots. *Besides, they're usually first-generation drivers.* The driver used his horn and a few Arab curses rather than his brakes while passing a truck stalled on the road. He passed on the right, leaving behind us a cloud of dust. "Lord," I prayed, "I know this is how most of the world drives, but I'd like to live a bit longer."

*   *   *

Sometimes risk comes because of other people's ignorance about us.

After dinner a rock came whizzing through our opened window. Another shattered the pane that remained closed. It scared me because Isaac was sleeping in that room. We rushed in to find shards of glass in Isaac's cradle, but he lay unharmed and still asleep. The rock throwers were the same kids who hit Tristan with a rock on the forehead two days before. But that night Mohammed was eating with us. He and I went out and talked to the kids. They were surprisingly sweet. They said they thought there was a witch in the basement of our place. They asked forgiveness and said they wouldn't do it again. But it could have been so different.

*   *   *

I don't like risk. But we risk because it's worth it. We risk because Jesus rewards risk.

Mike felt the need to encourage the believers and see if there were openings for the gospel. I felt concern for the fifteen students who would make the trip given the uncertainty of our reception by the villagers or Marxists Guerrillas in the area. But my concerns only heightened as our departure grew closer. As we loaded the pickup trucks, a messenger drove up to the clinic with a new report. There had been a landslide and the road we were to travel was impassable—we would have to pack it in. Mike said it meant hiking a bit longer—twelve hours longer—and we would have to hike across the landslide. Some students elected not to go. Within minutes another messenger arrived with more unsettling news: there had been an outbreak of cholera in a village we were to pass through, and two boys had died. A couple more students dropped out. I wasn't sure if I was watching the paring of Gideon's army, the first chapters of Job or a plain signal from God not to make the trip.

But Mike and I prayed with the Guatemalan leaders at the clinic, and we felt certain that God wanted us to go despite our fears. After saying sober goodbyes to my wife and three children, we left. The mudslide crossing was vertiginous but uneventful, and we saw no sign of cholera. The next day in the village of Sumalito, I saw two families give their lives to Christ.

*   *   *

Missions trips are inherently dangerous. We don't want people to risk foolishly, yet we don't want to spend our whole time on short terms worrying about safety either.

How much risk is acceptable? How do we define risk? How do we weigh risk? What is lost when we "manage" risk? What is lost when we don't risk?

Date sent:	Sun, 14 Jun 1998 17:01:23-0100
To:	Prayer Team
From:	Mack Stiles<Mack.Stiles@world.net.com>
Subject:	Antigua, Guatemala

Tomorrow we'll take school buses (locals call them chicken buses since folk also use them to transport livestock) and travel north to the Ixil area in the mountains of Guatemala. The place is remote, and the roads are dangerous, so please pray for us.

We've traveled them before, and over time I've learned that the biggest danger is not from bandits but from falling off the edge of the road. Even so, I've spent most of the day running from the police station to the keyboard and back again to supply the necessary documents (in Spanish) requesting an armed guard to accompany our bus. The police provided this service after the rape of four U.S. students on a tourist bus a couple of months ago. As I've sat in several governmental waiting rooms, I've had time to think about the missionary implications of "risk management." There seems to be a growing cultural view that safety is our highest value.

I don't think it's limited to the secular world either. Few of our students have been challenged to risk their lives for the sake of Jesus. Many pastors and Christian parents demand guarantees of safety that we are unable to give.

But those who live for safety alone end up living joyless lives. In his book *Culture of Fear* Frank Furedi says, "Those who propose avoiding risks and gaining safety will invariably find that what they acquire instead are obsessions."[1]

Furedi says that safety has become the fundamental value of our times. Passions that were once devoted to a struggle to change the world are now invested in trying to ensure that we are safe.

I agree, yet I'm arranging for armed transport because I don't want to take "unnecessary risk." That kind of risk we're not supposed to take—though no one ever tells us how to define it, it's amazing how little we do daily in modern life that is necessary.

Not taking unnecessary risk for us on this trip means trying to get the transport if I can, but if the transport doesn't show up tomorrow, I won't call off our trip. It's a decision that safety will not be our highest value. We believe we have a protector—that's why I'm writing—pray for us. As Furedi says, "When safety is worshipped and risks are seen as intrinsically bad, society is making a clear statement about the values that ought to guide life." [2] How true. I, for one, do not want to worship safety over God.

In Christ's care,

Mack Stiles

In one sense it is impossible to manage risk. We can't cover all the things that can go wrong. But we have seven things that must be kept in mind about risk.

1. Remember that Jesus rewards risk. Long before accountants noticed the market rewards risk, Jesus promised to reward those who risk for him (Mt 6:25-33).

2. Remember that there are no guarantees. Life is a risk. But take some simple precautions. Use safe airlines. Be in partnership with local people who can advise you on safety issues. Make sure all participants have good insurance.

3. All of life involves risk, but we don't look for risk either. Thrill seeking is not a part of missions. There are plenty of thrills on a missions trip without manufacturing them.

4. When you do need to risk, risk on things that are worth it. Sometimes that means spiritual realities the world simply cannot see; sometimes it means doing things that will build trust. Sometimes we eat risky food to build trust, for instance.

5. Manage risk by training yourself to do three things: be alert, be knowledgeable and be wise. Watch what is going on around you. What are the implications? Think through the things you can do to reduce risk at no expense to cultural sensitivity. Again, have partnerships with those who can guide you—remember that in crosscultural situations you are as lambs among wolves.

Have clear, wise rules for participants: in before dark; walk in groups; limit luggage, personal articles and spending money; don't flash your wealth; take cheap cameras—or do something really radical: leave your camera at home.

6. *When something bad happens—and something bad will happen—be calm and compliant.* Remember that there are no guarantees in life. That's true for a trip across the globe or down the street to the grocery store. When things do go wrong, give yourself a break. There's no sense heaping guilt on top of mistakes. Know that God is honored by your risk for him.

7. *Don't make the focus of your trip eliminating or managing risk.* What a boring trip. Don't make it the focus when you return either. We've endured too many short-term reports that focused entirely on how bad or dangerous or disgusting things were with no hint of God's work. We call them the "biggest bug" stories. No wonder so many short termers go and are surprised God was there before they were.

*   *   *

What goes around comes around. My father, a physician, made a commitment late in life to take early retirement from his practice to do missions work. We applauded his decision, though secretly we wondered if it would happen. But both Mom and Dad traveled with us to Kenya for a week to check out the hospital in Kijabe. That was twelve years ago. Today I'm wondering how Mom and Dad are doing on their sixth short term working at Bethany Children's Hospital. As I type, they've been gone for three months, and I'm worried about them. Dad is seventy years old; Mom is sixty-nine. I find myself fretting and feeling more compassion for Dr. Branham (who relented and let his daughter go despite the risks). It's risky. There are no guarantees. Yet I'm thrilled that my parents are becoming the people they want to be in Christ. You will too, if you take some risks.

17

Oh, the Places You Will Go
Families on Short Terms

FAX

To: First Alliance Kindergarten Sunday school class, c/o Mr. and Mrs. Cross

From: Tristan Stiles

Date: July 14, 1993

Re: Tristan says hello to his Sunday school class and to Mr. and Mrs. Cross.

I hope you are having a good summer. I had a good plane flight. I stopped at Amsterdam. We are having a good time here. It was 112 degrees last week. They worship Allah here, not Jesus. They pray really loud every day, even at night when we are asleep. I went to the beach today and found some shells.

Love, Tristan

The question people first ask us when they discover we spend most every summer on a short term is, "Do you take your children?" Though we puzzle over what other option we might exercise, we know that this question is a reflection many have about the rest of the world. But taking our children has been one of the greatest privileges within the great privilege of going on short terms: for us, our children and for crosscultural ministry.

For Us

There is nothing more disarming and vulnerable than people carrying their baby; it's hard to look mean. You may look tired or disheveled, but not mean. And in many cultures a person is not an adult until he or she has a child.

For Them

If we grow because of a short term, how much more do our children? Young children can pick up languages with amazing speed. Tristan would call out to me in Swahili "Kuja hapa, Baba" ("Come here, Daddy") after a week in Kenya. They also form friendships without being able to share a language (after all, they're still working on their mother tongue). They make fewer cultural mistakes (though even babies have cultural differences—I marvel at how good Japanese babies are!) Older children develop bigger views of the world. Tristan, even in kindergarten, began to have a heart for those who didn't know Jesus, those who worship other gods.

As they grow older, the experiences become richer and more difficult. Tristan has held dying children in his arms—children who died simply because they didn't get enough protein in their diets.

The questions are more difficult too.

"Dad?"

"Yes, Tristan," I said as we hiked from one small village to another.

"The church in Xoloche was raising money to put in some benches for their church, and I was just thinking about our church raising money for the air conditioner. How many benches do you think our air conditioner would buy?"

For Those to Whom We Minister

Children are people that all people understand. They become a point of connection that crosses cultures. Children are statements that we are willing to enter into someone else's culture fully and vulnerably.

When Ishmael and Henda came for dinner, Tristan produced his journal. He drew a picture of something he had seen each day. When people came over, he showed them his reflections of their country. Ishmael was so taken with Tristan's pictures that he drew one himself for the collection. The friendship that formed between the two was striking and a helpful door to friendship between our families.

Things to Remember

"But isn't it dangerous?" people ask us. We suppose it is. But today we find it more frightening that our children would be raised without having a bigger picture of the world than the one presented by the media. One of the best things about taking our children to other cultures is the bigger picture they have of the world. But the best is to minister as a family.

How to Prepare Your Kids

The best way to prepare your kids is to prepare yourself. Children are flexible, and they adapt well, but they will pick up your attitudes. If you have a hard time on the trip, they will too. Know your limitations. If travel is stressful for you at home, it will be in a foreign country. If you can't stand dust balls in the corner, you won't like sleeping on a dirt floor. That's not to say don't go, but be prepared to be flexible yourself.

You should also encourage flexibility with your children. When a sea creature was served for dinner in the Philippines, Tom and Nancy Brink's children asked what it was. Nancy's reply: "It's something new we're eating for dinner tonight," and the kids got it down better than the older short termers.

Directors and families need to communicate expectations before the trip begins. Some housing and food needs will be different for families. Some families are specific about their needs; others will be laid-back. Both directors and families should expect some unforeseen events to occur during the trip and be gracious and flexible in dealing with them. If you are the director, it's a good idea to take someone along to help with the kids.

Prepare your team as well. Ask the director to orient the group if possible: what ground rules do the kids have that the team needs to know about, for example. Give the team permission to jump in and help too. Always tell them to let the parents know if they want to take a child somewhere. (We've had a couple of panic attacks because we didn't tell the team about this one.)

Allow your kids to participate in the program as much as their age allows. Young children don't need much orientation; their main concern is where you are. The easiest children for us to take were babies (immobile), and the most difficult were our two year olds (mobile without understanding). Brief older children about what to expect. Have them take a stab at the language. They do better than adults. Encourage them to interact with the national children. Use this as an opportunity to build bridges with national families. Preteens and teens can actually enter into the mission. Ask for jobs they can do. Make sure to orient teens (assign this book) to crosscultural living.

Like you, they need to have some support systems in place. Get their Sunday school or youth group involved. Tristan's fax to the Sunday school helped the class pray for him. Have your children keep a journal. Even if they can't write, they can draw their experiences. Ask them what they are learning about themselves and their world.

Finally, take time to learn from them and how they see the new culture. Children's wide-eyed view of the world will help us see things we miss. Be ready to deal with hard questions and tough issues. Kids don't let them slip by as easily as adults. But they certainly have an easier time breaking down barriers and forming relationships.

We asked our Guatemala 98 team to split up into small groups for our debriefing time. Our family formed one small group. The questions were the same questions asked of everyone. I took notes of how Tristan (11) David (9) and Isaac (6) responded. These are my unedited notes of what our family learned.

☐ *What did God teach us this summer?*

Isaac: God is teaching us about love.

Tristan: Yes, we need to love one another, because without love we couldn't stay in small rooms together.

David: He's teaching us how to love people of other worlds. God says love those who curse you and pray for those who hate you.

Isaac: God is teaching us to teach around the world about Jesus.

David: We need to write down the songs we sang and teach them to the world.

☐ *What are we learning about ourselves?*

Tristan: I'm learning about patience.

Mom: I'm learning that God is faithful.

David: I'm learning about being nice and praising God.

Isaac: I'm learning how to pray at all times.

Tristan: I'm learning that faithful is a dog who always obeys his owner and is always there.

David: I think that since we've been with poor people and lived with poor people, we should always give food to poor people.

Tristan: We need to tell other families to do missions trips.

Isaac: I want to go to Russia.

Tristan: I want to go back to Kenya.

Dad: I think God is good.

We missed out on summer baseball, but it seems like a good trade to me.

18

Home Sweet Home?
Reentry

AFTER SPENDING SO MUCH TIME LEARNING AND STRIVING IN THE other culture, the return to a familiar place would seem to be easy. But for many, it is the most difficult part of the short-term experience. How can that be?

Cheeseburger, here I come! Despite three continents, eight time zones, four airplanes and a thirty-two-hour day, I couldn't wait.

I couldn't wait? When I got to JFK, I couldn't believe how busy everyone seemed. I hadn't seen anyone hurry that much all summer. The ticket agent seemed too busy for words. An angry businessman two people ahead of me began berating some people in line. *How rude,* I thought. I was definitely home, but I had forgotten some things.

Such as the wealth. Upon arrival our team was swept to a reception. An elegant reception: all that food! I couldn't help noticing the sharp contrast between the food and the barren kitchen of the Kenyan family we'd visited just a few days before in the slum—that food would go a long way toward feeding their eleven children. To make matters worse, because our flight was late, they started without us. They started without us! We'd been with people all summer that didn't start the party until *everyone* was there.

Then came the questions I learned to dread: "So, how was your summer?" Maybe I did put in too much detail. Twenty minutes later and midway through the second week, two friends excused themselves to get more punch. The third began catching me up on all the local news, including our church softball team. It seemed it had been a dismal season, but if I'd been there to play first base, she claimed, they would have done much better. *Good grief,* I thought. *How can I explain what I've been through to these people?*

It was then that I caught sight of Scott and Ruth, students who'd also gone on the trip, sitting by themselves in a corner. I overheard Ruth say she wanted to get right on a plane and go back to Kenya. My sentiments exactly.

I was experiencing reentry culture shock. And redlining at that—in my own home.

Reentry culture shock can be jolting. For openers, we are not expecting it. We expect to feel relieved to be returning to the familiar. Second, we tend to idealize home once we are away from it, especially when we see how the rest of the world lives. There are many privileges in being an American. When we are away, we focus on those and forget the bad. And last, our experience has changed us and some of these changes aren't known until we're confronted with how we live back home.

Returning to our home culture is a natural time to reassess how we fit in our society. Because we've seen and experienced a different way of doing things, we become conscious of attitudes and values we've never noticed before. We question them much more than we did before our *out-of-country* experience. There's conflict between our pre-trip self and our post-trip self. Everyone around us expects us to fit right back in and function as we always have, and yet some things just don't add up like they used to. This causes distress. We are back home, but we are still experiencing cultural dissonance—only this time it is with our own culture.

There are some common themes of tension in returning to American culture. Here are five we've heard most frequently from our students.

"I can't believe how materialistic everybody is." It is shocking how wealthy we are and how much we like and expect to own nice things. This is not unique to our culture. However, if you've been living in a developing nation or a country where goods are hard to get, you've become somewhat accustomed to doing without and found that lots of things you'd thought were necessary really aren't. You may have seen desperate poverty and need. Now back at home, malls and super-sized grocery stores are overwhelming, if not disgusting. Your home and possessions seem a lot nicer than they ever did before—maybe a little too nice. Everywhere around you, people are spending money, lots of it, on things that don't seem all that important anymore.

Before you went on your missions trip, you never thought about million-dollar building projects, velvet-covered pew cushions and resurfacing the parking lot every year. Now you begin to wonder who makes these decisions and what kind of priorities they have.

"None of my friends understand what I've been through." The

responses of our friends and family are mixed. Some, although interested in what we've been doing, have a difficult time picturing what our trip was like. It may be outside their realm of experience. Others are unimpressed or, worse, not interested.

Coupled with both reactions may be a sense of frustration at our inability to give people an accurate description of what happened and how we've changed. It's impossible to tell anyone who hasn't been to Kenya about what it is like to ride on a *matatu* or eat *ugali* or visit a *choo*. More difficult still is finding the right adjectives to communicate how our hearts were touched and our attitudes transformed.

"I've been preaching in churches all summer, and now my youth leader is wondering if I'm mature enough to lead a small group this fall." You may have had significant responsibility on your missions trip. Opportunities presented themselves, and you rose to the challenge. You know that you've really grown in using your spiritual gifts, but leaders here either don't know that or seem locked in a grid.

A similar frustrated feeling comes when you resume other roles or jobs. On your trip you've had incredible adventures and freedom. Now your parents want to know where you are going and when you'll be home. Your supervisor at work asks you to make a delivery and wonders if you can follow the street map.

"Americans are so naive about foreign countries and the issues involved; I'm beginning to think no one really cares." Front pages of our newspapers feature articles from the world of sports, but you must turn to an inside page to read one brief paragraph about Central America. Only seventh-grade social studies teachers know all the countries in Africa. We know more about Siam from *The King and I* than we do about modern Thailand. It seems as if Americans have little knowledge or concern about anything outside our borders.

Unfortunately, this inward focus is just as evident in many churches. While it is good to pray for our sick and for local events too, frequently we end there or pray only short, nebulous prayers for the rest of the world. Teaching about missions is often either nonexistent or dated.

"I've scarcely seen my roommates since I've been back, it seems like they're going a thousand miles an hour to a million different places!" Americans move at a frenetic pace. A successful day is often measured by how many things we are able to check off a list. Our events are neatly packaged into one-hour chunks. Heaven forbid that one of them should run over and interfere with our race to the next one.

Contrast this with what you experienced on your missions trip. You've been with a friendly, supportive team that allowed plenty of time to talk and get to know one another. You've spent hours in your host's homes drinking tea and waiting for the next event to occur, sometimes not knowing what it might be. At the beginning of the trip, your director asked you to be flexible, since things didn't always run efficiently or as expected, and you'd been compliant with her wishes. No car, no telephone, no e-mail, no fast food and no shopping malls can slow anyone down. You've become accustomed to an unhurried, single-focused schedule. Now it is very hard to readjust.

Perhaps you can't yet identify with any of these five disharmonies (maybe because you were on a missions trip to an affluent culture). Be sure and reread them when you return from your missions trip. It is quite normal to go through a confusing period when you reenter your home culture. There are several different reactions to this transitional time, and like relating crossculturally, some have a positive impact and some very negative.[1]

For most, unfortunately, coming home is no problem. After

some initial shock, they are able to separate their missions experience from the rest of their life. They did their *thing* for missions and the world. Now they can resume the pursuit of the American dream without much guilt.

Although they seem to have adjusted well, this mindset misses a tremendous opportunity for growth, both personal and spiritual. God wants us to share his heart for the lost and oppressed. The exposure we have to the disenfranchised during our trip stimulates an awakening or a deepening of our compassion. To set that aside is a wasted opportunity for ourselves as well as for those around us who may be stirred by our experience.

Other returnees have just the opposite reaction. They burn with righteousness and anger at all that is wrong with our country. When they see how naïve they were before their experience and how difficult it is to reprogram attitudes (both their own and others), they become depressed and cynical. Like the redliners discussed in an earlier chapter, they tend to withdraw and alienate.

A third response is a more healthy approach. These people are processing their experience and incorporating what they have learned about God and his world into their lives and bringing awareness to those around them.

Obviously, we'd all like to be in this last group. Here are some things you can do to help yourself choose this best option.

Make sure there is closure before you leave the mission field. Find out ways you can stay involved after you return home. Get information you need and figure out the best way to communicate. Complete as many of the tasks you've been given as you can. If this is impossible, organize them so it is easy for someone to come in and pick up where you left off. Take the time to say goodbye to people, both your hosts and your teammates.

Don't neglect to set aside time before you leave to reflect on the experience, both by yourself and with others. Review your expectations for the trip, how they were met or unmet, and the significance of these. For example, did God confirm that you are to return to the missions field? What steps will you take? Were you unable to interact with the national children like you wanted? Perhaps God allowed you to develop another gift or you learned a better way to approach children of this culture that will be valuable in the future.

There are other questions you'll want to reflect upon as well. What did you learn about God? What did you learn about yourself and how you relate to God and to others? What things stirred your heart? How have you been changed by this experience?

Prepare yourself for reentry. In his book *Re-Entry* Peter Jordan urges those returning from missionary service "to take time to properly assess how much you have changed, and how much things have changed back home. Never presume that no changes have occurred, even if you have only been away on a one-month outreach. Nothing stays the same, neither you nor the people you left at home."[2] Jordan goes on to suggest that we review different areas of our lives (physical, social, emotional, political, spiritual and financial) to determine how we've changed. If you kept a journal of your trip, this is a great time to review it, paying special attention to your emotions and ideas before you left and what you are feeling and thinking now.

It is also important to assess changes that have occurred at home and how they might affect your reentry. Perhaps your church has a new pastor, you need to find a job right away, or someone in your family has been diagnosed with a serious illness. The list could go on. What changes and concerns will you encounter when you enter into these situations? Prayerfully consider all these things.

Once home, be proactive *rather than* reactive. Just as when you entered your target culture, count on experiencing some unplanned emotions. You'll probably at some point be embarrassed, frustrated or confused. Good crosscultural skills are just as useful at those moments as they were on your missions trip. Commit yourself to working through relationships and situations at home in ways that lead to good communication and empathy.

It is also common to experience some downtime after such an exhilarating experience. You may feel that God is distant or that your trip didn't amount to anything. Remember that God is faithful here even as he was on the missions field. Reread your journal and remind yourself of the great things he did in your life and others' lives. Practice using the new gifts and areas of strength you developed in the other culture here at home in your church.

Be deliberate in providing yourself some more debriefing time. Processing of your experience doesn't end when you go through U.S. Customs. You need to set aside some time once home to continue to work through all you've been learning. This includes both time alone and with others. Face it, hardly any friends or family members are ready for a spontaneous four- to five-hour marathon conversation about your missions trip. We have found it helpful to have one or two highlight stories to tell to everyone and then set up an appointment to talk with two or three friends or mentors in greater depth.

In the midst of all this processing, pray that God would clarify the next steps of obedience for you. Continue to follow him by taking radical steps of faith just like you did when you agreed to go on the missions field in the first place. Finally, make sure you are involved with your church's missionary efforts at home. Help cross racial barriers. Reach out to international students. Help recruit or even direct a short term yourself.

Short Terms A—Z

This is a glossary of tips for short-term mission trips. It is not intended to be exhaustive; rather, we chose the words by brainstorm with a few short-term veterans. Some of these summarize what's in the first part of the book. Others are mentioned only here. We hope you find them helpful.

A

air travel. The face of missions has been changed by air travel (as opposed to boat travel) and made short-term missions feasible. The time spent on an airplane can be productive too: the chance to get to know your fellow teammates, have an interesting evangelistic conversation with the non-Christian sitting beside you, or to rest and pray to prepare yourself for your project or your return home.

airlines. We're not recommending one airline over another, but you should make your arrangements with a reputable travel agent who will book you with a reputable airline. One summer the airline we had ticketed went out of business while we were overseas; however because they were honest, they booked our group on another airline.

airplanes. Maybe you've never been on one, or maybe you've flown a lot. The personnel treat you pretty nice on these international flights: good food, movies, and they even help prepare you for customs by handing out the required forms to complete.

airport tax. Assessed in many countries, airport tax (or departure tax) is a fee you pay when you leave the country, often $20—$50. Typically, it must be paid in American dollars, so you need to learn the amount in advance so you can be certain to have the correct denominations.

animals. Remember that attitudes about animals in other cultures are different than ours. Often animals are livestock, not pets. Sometimes the livestock (chicken, pigs, goats) wander around freely; they may even be riding the bus with you!

anxiety. A normal response, anxiety often occurs when you're preparing to step into something unknown. Don't let it get out of hand. Take Paul's advise in Philippians 4:6-7.

B

baggage. Take as little as possible. Remember, it is likely you'll be carrying the baggage yourself everywhere you go, so make sure you can. I suggest one suitcase or duffel and a day pack. Practice carrying them (fully packed) around the block before you leave, then unpack nonessential items. I have noticed a correlation with anxiety and baggage weight. The more stuff, the greater the anxiety levels.

begging. Many developing countries will have beggars. Don't let complexity of poverty overrule a heart of compassion. Don't forget, we *are* wealthy (we wouldn't be there if we weren't). Find ministries and churches that work with the poor and support them.

biblical basis of missions. See chapters three and four. For further study look up these passages: *God's universal concern:* Genesis 1:1; 1:25-28; 6:5-13; 9:1-7; 11:1-9; Psalm 33:6-9; 67; 96; Philippians 2:5-11; *God's purpose for Israel:* Genesis 12:1-7; 26:1-6; 28:10-16; Exodus 9:13-16; 19:1-8; Joshua 4:19-24; Judges 2:1-23; Isaiah 48:17-22; *God's personal interaction with humankind through the ministry of Jesus:* Matthew 8:5-13; 22:41-49; Mark 1:32-34; 7:24-30; Luke 4:16-21; 5:29-32; 7:36-50; John 1:14; 4:7-30. What Jesus said: Matthew 28:16-20; Mark 16:14-18; Luke 24:33-49; John 20:19-21; Acts 1:6-12; Philippians 2:5-11; *God's purpose for the church:* John 17:14-26; Acts 1:8; 6:1-7; 8:1-8; 13:1-5; Romans 3:19-30; 10:9-17; 15:7-21; 1 Corinthians 9:19-22; 12:19-30; 2 Timothy 2:2; 1 Peter 2:9-10; Revelation 7:9-17. [1]

bonding. We form strong ties with those we spend time with, especially on our initial entry. Sometimes it is easier to bond with fellow short termers so you'll need to be intentional in spending time with nationals and developing friendships. This can be the most rewarding part of a short-term project: to form a bond of friendship with a national person.

bribes. Gaining special treatment through payment of money or favors, a bribe is different from but often confused with extortion (requiring payment for a service that is your due). For example, a bribe: "For a small gift, Mr. Stiles, I can seat your group in first class." Extortion: "Mr. Stiles, I'm afraid that we are going to have to inspect your group's luggage; it will take us an hour to do that, and since your flight leaves in thirty minutes, it looks like you'll miss this week's plane ... Now for a small fee ..."

It is a common way of doing business in some cultures for low-paid civil servants, but don't resign yourself to sacrificing your integrity. Ask questions, appeal to a higher authority, or talk to a long-term missionary about the best way to handle this.

buses. Going by bus is the more common way to travel in country. Prepare to be crowded.

C

CDC. The Centers for Disease Control and Prevention (CDC) is a U.S. government agency that can provide accurate information about the health concerns and recommendations for your target country. Their phone number is (877) 394-8747. They can be reached at <www.cdc.gov> on the Web.

clothing. Be culturally sensitive when it comes to choosing clothing (see chapter nine). In addition, remember that you may do your own washing by hand, so take things that are easy to wash and dry. Don't take anything that you expect to bring back in perfect shape. Travel clothing is usually very practical; there are many travel catalogues and camping equipment stores that carry easy-care clothing.

coping skills. Tools such as coping skills help you move through culture shock in a healthy, relationship-building way. Some examples are making observations, asking questions and trying new things (see chapter eleven).

culture shock. If you're trying to be involved with your host culture,

culture shock is unavoidable. Negative feelings don't mean you're being ungodly but your response needs to be one that invites relationship rather than shutting it down (see chapter ten).

custom agents. Although not usually out to *get* you, custom agents do have a difficult job. Be polite, cooperative and unassuming. Remember that you are in their country and need to obey their laws.

customs forms. You will be asked to fill out customs forms when you enter and leave a country and before you reenter your own country. They ask questions like where you are staying and how long you'll be there, what you are bringing in or out of the country. Read the directions carefully. Your short-term director may give you information about how to complete these.

D

declaring. We go to declare Jesus, but it doesn't hurt to support the local economy while you are there. You will have to declare your purchases over a certain dollar amount on a form when you reenter your home country.

diarrhea. A fact of crosscultural living, international visitors get diarrhea when they visit our country too. Drink extra fluids (from a safe source such as bottled water or beverages or drinks that have been boiled), get plenty of rest and use good sense about what you consume. I often pack powdered Gatorade or some such electrolyte-replacement beverage. Seek medical advice if your stool is bloody or foul-smelling, or if you have severe cramps. These may be signals of dysentery.

directing. To direct a short term is a rewarding, if challenging, privilege. Crosscultural living and its unique advantage of taking away some of our normal props and coping mechanisms opens many opportunities for ministry in the lives of our teammates.

dress. What may be very appropriate and accepted dress in our country may not be in other places. Remember that your goal is not to express your individuality. As foreigners we will stick out anyway; there's no need to accentuate this. Try to err on the side of conservative rather than seeing how far you can push the limit (see chapter nine).

drinking water. In many countries we do need to be careful about our drinking water but not offensive about it. Don't alienate your host with an insulting reply when they have kindly offered you refreshment. Point to your own frailty as our Kenyan friend, Philip Kishoyian, did when he introduced our short termers into a new African home, "Remember, these Americans have weak stomachs and will need to have their water boiled." Use good sense too. I've seen many short termers be diligent about drinking bottled water in restaurants but then pour it into a glass full of ice from an unknown source.

dysentery. A serious form of diarrhea, dysentery is usually caused by an infection, either bacterial or amebic.

E

eating. Be wise but also be sensitive, especially if your host has prepared the food for you. Often they have given you their best or have been overly generous with what little they have. We had some short termers refuse to eat a family's only chicken, which had been slaughtered in their honor (see chapter nine).

emergencies. All directors should have contingency plans and know how to reach the American embassy. Someone responsible back home should have a list of all participants and emergency-contact information. This person should also know exactly how to reach the director should a stateside family emergency occur.

event oriented. Some cultures emphasize the event rather than the time consumed. For example, in an event-oriented culture a church service would continue until all the plans had been completed, even if that meant running over the time allotment (see chapter nine).

expectations. Conscious or subconscious, expectations may be concrete or vague. This is not a bad thing. We all have hopes and dreams for our missions trip. However, we feel frustrated when our expectations are not met. Use this time of frustration to evaluate your assumptions and be open to the fact that God may have a very different agenda.

F

finances. Most short-term missions trips require you to raise money before you go. Your director should inform you of the amount needed and may give you a breakdown of how that money will be spent. There may be some extra expenses not included in this fee; you'll need to find out what these are and how much they will cost. Some examples are passport and visa fees, immunizations, books, and domestic travel. You'll also want to have some spending money for the trip. (Consider leaving in the country the money you don't spend.)

Remember, fundraising can be a wonderful way to experience the care of the church body. It can also engender prayer support.

flexibility. The mantra of crosscultural living is flexibility. Not only is everything done differently, but even the best laid strategy may not work. We need to adapt to whatever situation presents itself instead of focusing on our spoiled plans.

food. You will be expected to eat things you've never had before. Be adventurous with your palate. Don't become the ugly American tourist who insists that he or she be fed American food (see chapter nine). McDonald's is found the world around, but try to avoid it. Experience local food and eat at McDonald's when you get home.

frame of reference. The sum of a person's experience, beliefs and worldview constitutes our frame of reference. We speak out of our own frame of reference, but our words are interpreted by another person's frame of reference. We need to understand how those two frames are different to communicate well (see chapter nine).

G

game parks and other tourist attractions. We've seen groups of tourists so decked out in their safari clothes and gear that they are more interesting to watch than the animals. Tourist attractions can be very interesting but also can be a distraction to why you go. See if those people you are ministering to go to these places and then plan your trip accordingly.

gift giving. One universal expression of friendship is gift giving—if given in a way appropriate in the culture. You'll have to figure out the appropriate manner, otherwise the gift may not be well received. For example, in Kenya it was important to give a gift of a toy to the family (the parents) rather than the individual child because all the children in the family and perhaps in the neighborhood would share the toy.

greenlining. Greenlining means developing understanding, empathy and rapport with a culture after experiencing culture shock by using good crosscultural coping skills (see chapter eleven).

guitars. A practical instrument to bring on a short term, guitars not only can accompany your group's worship times, but they can be a bridge to start a conversation, gather a crowd or to learn music of your host culture. This same thing will be true of any instrument you can bring on the trip. We had one student who brought her flute and played frequently for groups of children. You might want to bring an inexpensive one and plan to leave it with your hosts.

H

Hallelujah! Praise the Lord! A word never needing translation. You will have many reasons to praise God as you see his faithfulness, love and power when you step into another culture.

healing prayers. Although they may be foreign to your church background, healing prayers are offered frequently in the New Testament and may be a common practice of the national church of your host country. You'll probably send up a few of your own (see *diarrhea*).

health. We tell our groups, "Let us relieve your anxiety about getting sick; you're going to get sick, so don't worry about it." Given travel, different diets and time changes, you'll have a day when you don't feel well. Remember, it could happen at home too. Most illness is limited to stomach upset or diarrhea. Don't try to tough it out. If you feel badly, let people know. Do act wisely: don't expose yourself to unnecessary risk and make sure your immunizations are current and the correct ones for your target country. (Go to <www.cdc.gov> for a full listing of a listing of disease and health topics.)

homesickness. Being in a radically different place will make us all long for the familiar. Homesickness can come in odd ways and at unexpected times. Your family and home may seem very far away. If you experience it, tell a kind teammate or your director. Sometimes it is helpful just to talk to someone about your family and your home life.

home-stay tips. Although there are too many home-stay tips to list here, living with a national family will be a careful test of your crosscultural attitude and skills. Take advantage of this unique opportunity. Get to know the whole family. Participate in family life as much as you are able. This is a treasure.

humor. You'll need a good sense of humor when living crossculturally. You'll want to keep a good sense of humor about yourself and all the mistakes you'll make. Laughter dispels tension. Make sure your jokes are not at the expense of your hosts or their culture. Americans tend to be loud and boisterous, which is not always taken well in other cultures, so be sensitive about this.

I

indigenous people. An anthropological term, indigenous people are those who originate from or have consistently lived in a certain region. They have a distinct culture that may be slightly or radically different from the mainstream culture of the big city.

insects and other bugs. Of course we have insects at home too, but if you are living in a rustic setting, you may see more than you are used to. Like a good fishing story, they seem to grow larger with time and distance.

internationals. You are an international when you go to another country. Use your experience when you return home to help you empathize with visitors to our culture. Treat them as you would like to have been treated on your missions trip.

J

jet lag. Air travel is a wonderful thing, but it often gets us to our destination before our body rhythms can catch up. Signs of jet lag are fatigue, irritability and strange dreams. Set your watch to the new time when you first depart. Get your mind working in the new time zone even as you travel. If you have crossed a number of time zones, take it easy on yourself the first couple of days. Don't pack too much into your schedule. To adjust as quickly as possible, you must get your old time zone out of your head and follow the schedule of the new time zone. (That is, eat at the proper mealtimes and sleep during *their* night, not during your nighttime back home.)

journal. Perhaps the most valuable thing you can do for yourself during your trip is to keep a journal. Journals are a good friend to *talk* to when you are feeling confused or lonely. They can help you see how God is speaking to you; they can record memories you don't want to forget; they can help you process what you are learning and hold you accountable to changes you intend to make in your attitude or lifestyle. They are helpful when you go back home and want to tell everyone about your experience. Even if you are not a good diary keeper or writer, you'll want to keep a record of your missions trip in your own words.

justice. Justice is a hard thing to deal with in another culture because what you will find, more likely, is *injustice.* Many people groups have been marginalized. Not every country has a bill of rights or practices due process, which guarantee freedoms we assume in our culture. Minister to those God has put in your path with his gifts of love and mercy. If you can't change the situation, maybe you can change the lives of a few people (see chapter twelve).

K

kids, of hosts. Kids are naturally curious and are a fairly nonthreatening entry into the culture. Get to know them and their families. Be careful to understand how children and adults interact in other cultures before you assume that hosts interact the same as at your home. Be careful about gift giving, carrying children and allowing children on work sites that may be dangerous (for more on families see chapter seventeen).

kids, your own. Your own kids (or those included in your program) are also great icebreakers. Use them to begin conversations and relationships. Don't forget to include them in programs and, when appropriate, on work sites.

kindness. Something you should consciously extend during a missions trip is kindness. You are not the only one feeling stressed. Your director, teammates, missionary coordinator or national coordinator may be refreshed by a kind word or gesture. Be considerate of your hosts as well.

L

LAMP. Language Acquisition Made Practical (LAMP)[2] is a language-learning method that is very effective and integrates a person into the culture. The student spends much time in public, trying to make conversation with people and so practicing and expanding his or her language abilities.

language. Learn a language from nationals. Find a friend who will help. Language school can be a good investment of your time especially to learn a few key phrases and greetings. Check out locations and ratings in some of the travelers' guidebooks available at your library or local bookstore.

laughter (*see* humor). Laughter is a good antidote to taking yourself too seriously. Part of culture shock is not always knowing when something is funny, or when it is or isn't a good time to laugh, or wondering if you are the object of amusement.

living conditions. Varied even within the same missions trip, some living conditions will be rugged, others nicer than what you are used to at home. The rule here is to be flexible and try to build bridges of trust with your host.

local transportation. Something you won't want to miss is the local transportation. It can be a great adventure and taste of the culture. Use local transportation when you can. Driving around in a car is more efficient and comfortable, but it isolates you from the culture.

long terms. A long-term missions trip is generally considered three years or more. You should try to meet some long-term missionaries who work in your area. They can give you helpful observations about the culture and are fascinating people.

M

mail. A letter from home can be encouraging, so urge your family and friends to write if you have an address. If your group is too mobile for an address, sometimes e-mail, faxes and telephones are available. There are many Internet bars popping up in tourist centers where, for a fee, you can send e-mail. Remind your family that mail is slow, and you probably can't communicate with them as efficiently as you do at home.

manual labor. We've never worked as hard as on some of our short-term projects. In developing nations much of the labor is still done by hand. If your project involves labor, plan on working hard and volunteer to learn things you've never done before. For example, Leeann helped build a fifty-yard sidewalk, including stairs, and even mixed the cement by hand.

medicines. There is no need to be a walking drug store, but basic first-aid supplies are useful. If you take a prescription medicine regularly, try to get a supply that will last through the end of your trip. Write down the generic name of that and any medications you may need, as the brand names change from country to country.

money. Often Americans think they can fix something simply by pouring money into it. This is usually not true in crosscultural settings. Be generous, but at the same time find culturally appropriate ways to give your money. Money can be very destructive, so make sure, when dealing with larger sums of money, you are working with agencies and not individuals.

music. Unique but integral to each culture is its music. It may sound strange to your ears; your music may sound strange to them in return. Listen carefully. You may want to record some to play when you return home as a reminder of your trip.

N

nationals. Citizens or members of a society are known as nationals. This is the appropriate term to use.

O

observation skills. Something you'll want to sharpen and use when you enter a culture are your observation skills. Being observant helps you learn how to act so that you build bridges of trust (see chapter eleven).

P

packing. It is tempting to pack everything you think you may possibly need. Resist this temptation. Not only will you wind up with a lot of heavy baggage to haul around, you may be embarrassed at your extravagant abundance compared to your host's humble existence (unless your missions trip is to Japan or Abu Dhabi). Westerners can all learn to live with less. Keep clothing down to three or four outfits; leave appliances like hair dryers at home (they may not work with the local current anyway); don't take a lot of things to do; rather, plan on spending time with your hosts.

parents. Your parents may or may not be supportive of what you are intending to do. It is a big step for them too, especially if you are still living with them. Keep them informed about your decisions and plans. Let them read all the information you receive before the trip. Write them while you are away to let them know how and what you are doing. Having your parents go is more difficult, but remember that they're adults, be supportive. Parents and children going together is a great thing to do.

passports. If you don't have one, apply for a passport as soon as possible. They may take up to six weeks to process. Get an application form from the main post office in your town. You'll also need your birth certificate, two passport photos (which have specific requirements that most photo studios know), an ID (such as a driver's license) and a check or cash for the amount specified on the application. Directors should have a photocopy of everyone's passport.

PDA. In many cultures, public display of affection is taboo. It reflects poorly on those involved (particularly on the woman) and your group. Caution is required even in gestures you consider meaningless (like a pat on the back). On the other hand, affection between two members of the same sex may be common: men holding hands or women walking arm in arm. Again, talk with hosts.

photography. Don't spend so much time behind the lens of your camera that it becomes the person your hosts know rather than the real you. Ask permission before photographing individuals or groups, particularly children. Some traditional groups may feel offended by cameras; you need to respect this. Remember that in many countries, public areas like the airports or railway stations are part of the national defense system and may not be photographed. *Never* photograph police, military personnel, weapons, police stations or defense installations. If you do, your camera may be confiscated and the film destroyed, and you could end up in jail. And remember, looking at people through a lens of a camera doesn't build trust but confirms that we're really there to be tourists.

PQT. A prior question of trust (PQT) means to ask yourself if what you are thinking, doing or saying is building or undermining trust. It is an essential step in moving crossculturally well (see chapter nine).

prayer partners. A valuable part of short terms is to have prayer partners. Your risks are spiritual as well as physical, so have some people praying for you. They can also hold you accountable in your preparation and reentry. We have had short termers send postcards to prayer partners during the trip, which was very helpful.

prep. The most important prep is spiritual, so don't neglect your devotions and prayer life in the months and weeks before you depart. Take the time to read your materials and do the things your director requires before you leave.

Q

quiet times. Quiet times or devotional times are crucial during the trip as well. Remember that you are the fulfillment of God's plan, not your own plan, so you need to stay in touch with him.

R

redlining. Responding to cultural difference by rejecting the culture is called redlining. It leads to isolation and alienation. If you suddenly find yourself redlining, pray for God to give you a new insight, a fresh perspective or just plain guts to keep pushing for relationship rather than estrangement (see chapter eleven).

reentry. Many surprises await you on your reentry here because you will be a changed person, having lived much life in the course of a very short time, while people back home have been about their normal routine. This is a time to process, set some goals for your changed life and begin to act upon them (see chapter eighteen).

respect. The concept of respect is not just a good idea but an expectation in many cultures. Few cultures are as egalitarian as ours. In general, older persons and officials should be treated respectfully. Use your cultural observation skills to determine who else is honored in your host culture.

romance. It is exciting when short-term participants from our missions trips write us to say they have decided to marry one another. I received a phone call as I typed this section that Aaron and Tracy, who met in Guatemala, are getting married and want Mack to perform the ceremony. But at the beginning of each trip we ask that there be no romance. Why? Because the trip will be a focused, intense time, and we hate for anyone to miss what God has for them. Romance is distracting and takes lots of time. If you think you've met the *one* on your trip, remember two things: first, if it is true love, it will last until you get home; and second, a missions trip can be deceivingly romantic. This perfect person may not be so wonderful a few months down the road, and you've wasted a good portion of this special opportunity flirting with him or her.

ROS. A retreat of silence (ROS) is an extended time spent by yourself with the Lord. It is a time to reflect and prepare for a next step. We have two ROS's (of about three hours in length) on our missions trips, one at the beginning to prepare our spirits for ministry and one at the end to reflect on God's faithfulness and what he would have for us next.

S

sermons. You may be asked to give one if you are to be a part of the host church. Start with a simple passage of Scripture you know well, explain it in your own words and tell how it can be applied. Add a story that can be understood by all cultures. Keep it simple. Remember, translations make a sermon twice as long. In choosing your illustrations, make sure you consider the experience of your audience and tailor it to a situation they would understand (*see* frame of reference).

servanthood. True servanthood is modeled by Jesus. We want to have this attitude too.

shopping. While we do want to support the national economy, shopping easily becomes a way of escaping the culture rather than embracing it. Remember that the purpose of your trip is not to collect exotic treasures but to share the love of Christ.

short-term missions trips. A short-term missions trip is usually under two years. For the purposes of this book they are typically measured in weeks and months, not years.

Short-Term Missions Today. An extremely helpful annual magazine with information, opportunities and resources for short terms. The listing of short-term missions books alone is worth the magazine. Contact Bill Berry at <Bberry4215@aol.com> or write to *Short-Term Missions Today*, P.O. Box 40519, Pasadena, CA 91114.

support raising. Contrary to popular opinion, support raising is a good thing. It is not only biblical (Paul did lots of fundraising), but it gives your family, friends and church the opportunity to become involved with you. You are not asking for a handout but instead giving them a chance to be generous and share in the work of Christ. Remember to thank them for donations and keep them informed about your trip.

T

team. There is no one else on earth who will understand your experience like those on your team. Missions trips are a bonding experience because they are so unique and intense. Make the most of these relationships. Part of your going may be to learn something about God through another teammate or for you to be God's comforter in another teammate's experience.

teammates. Although they are wonderful, teammates can also be a thorn in the flesh. Remember everyone is feeling the same cultural stress you are but may be expressing it in different (obnoxious?) ways. This would be a good time to work on the fruit of the Spirit: "patience, kindness, goodness, faithfulness, gentleness and self-control" (Gal 5:22-23).

telephones. Telephones may or may not be available. Be careful about making promises to call family or friends back home; it will only worry them when you don't. Public phones are sometimes available at the post office or center of town; however, they may be horrendously expensive. International calling cards can be very helpful, but watch out for rip-offs and scams.

testimony. Have your testimony prepared but be adaptable. At one Kenyan church service, Leeann was prepared to give her testimony. She heard her name called, grabbed her notes and started toward the platform when the next line of the translation came through. It was then she discovered that she would be singing a solo instead—the first one of her life. Fortunately, she happened to know the song announced. Even if you are participating in a work project, you should "be prepared to give an answer to everyone who asks you to give the reason for the hope that you have" (1 Pet 3:15). Practice your testimony before you go. Make sure it is concise and points to Jesus, not yourself.

time changes (*see* jet lag). Dealing with time changes can make you feel weird for a few days, unfortunately, right upon your arrival, which is a key time for forming relationships. Note the recommendations for jet lag and pray that the God of all times will give an extra measure of strength and grace.

time oriented. The term *time oriented* describes a person or group placing a high value on timekeeping (usually thought of as the opposite of event oriented). Being prompt, efficient and holding to a schedule are important to these folk. Western culture is time oriented; many other cultures are not (see chapter nine).

translator. Using a translator takes some getting used to. It is helpful to give him or her any information you can beforehand, such as Scripture texts, illustrations and visual aides. Speak slowly and break after every short sentence or phrase.

travel agents. Good travel agents can make your life simple by taking care of all those details you'd rather not. Bad ones can bring on a migraine. Things to look for are availability of your agent, attention to detail, prompt service, bookings with reputable airlines and a concern to find you the best fare possible.

U

umbrella strollers. When traveling with small kids, umbrella strollers are great.

understanding. Attaining understanding crossculturally is more difficult but very rewarding when it happens. It is an important part of building a trusting relationship.

unwritten codes of conduct. An embarrassing part of cultural dissonance occurs when all your hosts know how to act and you don't due to some unwritten code of conduct. Remember to use your observation skills, ask questions and resist the temptation to freeze and shut down. Try to put what you learn into practice the next time the situation occurs.

Urbana Student Mission Convention. Known more frequently as simply *Urbana*, the Urbana Student Mission Convention is InterVarsity Christian Fellowship's triennial missions convention held in Urbana, Illinois. Urbana is a great place to learn about missions and make contact with missions opportunities, both short- and long-term. Get more info from <www.urbana.org>.

U.S. embassy. It's a good idea to know where the U.S. embassy is in case you have a problem with your passport or visa. If you are a director, you should let the embassy know that you have a group in the country. These are your tax dollars at work and can be a helpful resource for you.

V

Vacations with a Purpose. Vacations with a Purpose is a great group with wonderful resources for your short-term ministry team—including the book *Vacations with a Purpose* by Chris Eaton and Kim Hurst.

Vaccinations (*see* CDC). Immunizations may be required to enter another country. Check on these early in your preparation as some are a series of two or three and must be separated by a few weeks. Your local health department can administer these or tell you where you can get them. They should also provide you with a world health card to be shown at customs.

W

water. Don't act neurotic about the water but do be wise. Ask hosts about the water. You can trust boiled water and drinks that have been boiled. We use a water filter with great success. And Coke is ubiquitous.

water conserving. Utilities are not always as consistent and unlimited as we're used to. For example, when we lived in Ngong, Kenya, we only had water on Tuesday and Thursday. We filled a large barrel in the kitchen to keep us until the next time. Be sensitive and conservative. Be willing to forgo your nightly hot bath.

wealth. In most parts of the world you will be thought to have a lot of wealth. After all, you're an American, you've traveled all this way, and you have a lot of stuff with you. You may be asked for money, even for large sums. Don't be offended. Try to be generous and look for ways you can help meet long-term needs. If you decide to give money, find out the culturally appropriate way to do it.

weather. Elevation as well as latitude can affect climate. You'll want to research what the weather will be like before you decide what to pack. Even if you are visiting a temperate climate, there may not be heat in the homes; nights can get chilly. Our coldest summer ever was in Nairobi—and we thought all of Africa was hot.

work projects. A work project is a type of short-term mission that focuses on a labor-intensive project such as building a church. Plan to develop lots of new muscle on these, as most of the work will be by hand. Even though the focus is on completing a task, be prepared to take opportunities you have to share the gospel. Get involved with the local church while you are there.

X

xenophobia. A fear or hatred of foreigners is called xenophobia. If you are reading this book, it is unlikely that you have a severe case of it, but we all must prayerfully look at ourselves and ask God to help us get rid of our bias toward different people.

x-ray machines. Although x-ray machines are common in every airport, sometimes you will be frisked in addition. These checks are for your protection. Accept them with a spirit of cooperation. Resistance will arouse suspicions and can get you in a heap of trouble. Most modern x-ray machines will not damage film, but some older models will fog high-speed film.

Y

youth hostels. See a travel guide for listings. Youth hostels may be a creative place to stay overseas.

Z

zoo. A zoo is the place to go if you want to see exotic animals—not a short-term missions trip.

Notes

Chapter 1: The Risky Adventure
[1]Kenyan staples of ground hominy and mixed greens.

Chapter 3: Abraham's Math Lesson
[1]John Piper, *Let the Nations Be Glad* (Grand Rapids, Mich.: Baker, 1993), p. 11.

Chapter 4: Models for Modern Short Terms
[1]See STEM research at <www.stemmin.com>.
[2]F. F. Bruce, *Paul: Apostle of the Heart Set Free* (Grand Rapids, Mich.: Eerdmans, 1978), p. 475.
[3]Most modern missions consider a short term any trip under two years.
[4]Scott Bessenecker, "Paul's Short-Term Church Planting: Can It Happen Again?" *Evangelical Missions Quarterly*, July 1997, pp. 326-32.

Chapter 5: Short Terms with a Long-Term View
[1]Paul wanted the new Gentiles believers to know they didn't have to become Jewish to be followers of Christ.

Chapter 6: Extra!
[1]Elisabeth Elliot, *Through Gates of Splendor* (Wheaton, Ill.: Tyndale House, 1981); and *Shadow of the Almighty* (San Francisco: HarperSanFrancisco, 1989).
[2]Elisabeth Elliot, *Shadow of the Almighty* (Grand Rapids, Mich.: Zondervan, 1958), p. 245.
[3]Elisabeth Elliot, "The Glory of God's Will," 1976 Urbana Student Mission Convention address. Though her talk during Urbana 96 was equally challenging, this quote comes from her address at Urbana 76 twenty years earlier.

Chapter 7: A God for All the Potatoes
[1]D. Guthrie, J. A. Motyer, A. M. Stibbs and D. J. Wiseman, eds., *The New Bible Commentary*, rev. ed. (Grand Rapids, Mich.: Eerdmans, 1984), pp. 91-92.
[2]Derek Kidner, *Genesis*, Tyndale Old Testament Commentaries (London: Tyndale Press, 1967), p. 110.

Chapter 8: Kenyan House-Help
[1]This story first appeared in J. Mack Stiles, *Speaking of Jesus* (Downers Grove, Ill.: InterVarsity Press, 1995), pp. 80-89.

Chapter 9: Questions of Trust
[1]This gives understanding to a number of passages of Scripture, such as Abraham's conversation with Ephron the Hittite in Genesis as he buys a burial plot for his wife, Sarah (Gen 23:10-16).
[2]Marvin K. Mayers, *Christianity Confronts Culture* (Grand Rapids, Mich.: Zondervan,

1974), p. 32.

[3]This concept has enormous implications for sharing the gospel with anyone. We should always be asking the prior questions of trust in evangelistic discussions.

[4]E. Thomas and Elizabeth S. Brewster, *Language Learning Is Communication—Is Ministry?* (Pasadena, Calif.: Lingua House, 1984).

[5]This is an impossible standard to maintain since the cultural anthropologist's mere presence changes culture.

Chapter 10: Culture Shock!
[1]*Ma* is the tribal language of the Masai people.

Chapter 12: Scars
[1]Gary Haugen, *Good News About Injustice* (Downers Grove, Ill.: InterVarsity Press, 1999), p. 69.

[2]That is, in white church culture. This is familiar territory in the African American church.

Chapter 13: Headlines from Mombasa
[1]Contextualization delineates between missionary's cultural mindset, host's cultural mindset and, though not often noted, biblical cultural mindset, with the intent to share truths of the gospel in the mindset of the host, without doing damage to meaning. It is much harder to do than to define.

[2] Winfried Corduan, *Neighboring Faiths* (Downers Grove, Ill.: InterVarsity Press, 1998), p. 40.

Chapter 14: Partnerships
[1]That is, insofar as we are willing to submit to their leadership or role model and not try to simply impose Western models into their situation. See previous chapter on contextualization.

Chapter 15: Pith Helmets & Modern Missionaries
[1]Native Guatemalans who are Mayan descendants.

[2]These quotes come from a talk given by Elisabeth Elliot at a seminar at the 1976 Urbana Student Mission Convention.

Chapter 16: Unnecessary Risk?
[1]Frank Furedi, *Culture of Fear: Risk-Taking and the Morality of Low Expectations* (Herndon, Va.: Cassell Academic, 1997), p. 12.

[2]Ibid., p. 4.

Chapter 18: Home Sweet Home?
[1]Linda Olson, "Towards Growthful Reentry," in *Student Training in Missions Manual* (Madison, Wis.: InterVarsity Christian Fellowship, 1992), pp. 31-32.

[2]Peter Jordan, *Re-Entry: Making the Transition from Missions to Life at Home* (Seattle: Youth With a Mission Publishing, 1992), pp. 42-43.

Short Terms A—Z
[1]Olson, *Student Training in Missions Manual*, pp. 14-15.

[2]E. Thomas Brewster and Elizabeth Brewster, *Language Acquisition Made Practical* (Pasadena: Lingua House, 1984).